GOD'S KINDNESS HAS OVERWHELMED US

A CONTEMPORARY DOCTRINE OF THE JEWS AS THE CHOSEN PEOPLE

Emunot: Jewish Philosophy and Kabbalah

Series Editor
Dov Schwartz (Bar-Ilan University)

Editorial Board
Ada Rapoport-Albert (University College, London)
Gad Freudenthal (C.N.R.S, Paris)
Gideon Freudenthal (Tel Aviv University)
Moshe Idel (Hebrew University, Jerusalem)
Raphael Jospe (Bar-Ilan University)
Ephraim Kanarfogel (Yeshiva University)
Menachem Kellner (Haifa University)
Daniel Lasker (Ben-Gurion University, Beer Sheva)

God's Kindness Has Overwhelmed Us

A CONTEMPORARY DOCTRINE OF THE JEWS AS THE CHOSEN PEOPLE

Jerome (Yehudah) GELLMAN

Boston 2013

Library of Congress Cataloging-in-Publication Data:
A catalog record for this title is available from the Library of Congress.

Copyright © 2013 Academic Studies Press All rights reserved

ISBN 978-1-61811-170-8 (Cloth)
ISBN 978-1-61811-192-0 (Electronic)

Book design by Adell Medovoy

Published by Academic Studies Press in 2013
28 Montfern Avenue
Brighton, MA 02135, USA
press@academicstudiespress.com
www.academicstudiespress.com

הַלְלוּ אֶת יְיָ כָּל גּוֹיִם שַׁבְּחוּהוּ כָּל הָאֻמִּים, כִּי גָבַר עָלֵינוּ חַסְדּוֹ....

All nations praise God! All peoples extol Him! For his kindness has
overwhelmed us....
—Psalms: 117

בֵּינִי וּבֵין בְּנֵי יִשְׂרָאֵל אוֹת הִוא לְעֹלָם
Between Me and the Children of Israel it is a sign "to the world"
—Exodus 31:17

Dedicated, with honor and love,
to the Jewish Sabbath
"Shabbos"

Table of Contents

Acknowledgements

This book was written under the auspices of the Van Leer Institute in Jerusalem, in a workshop on Jewish thought under the direction of Dr. Moshe Meir. I am most grateful to Moshe Meir and Van Leer for this affiliation. My deepest gratitude goes to the members of my Van Leer discussion group, Rabbi Tamar Elad-Appelbaum, Dror Bondi, Adam Danel, Alik Isaacs, and Asa Kedar. Their intellectual impressiveness and spiritual sensibilities were invaluable to me. May they be blessed with all that is good.

I am indebted to many others for their help and support in this project. No writer can wish for a better reader than Jonathan Malino. His philosophical acumen was greatly appreciated. Yotam Benzamin carefully read a previous version of this work and provided valuable criticism. Rabbi Nathan Lopez Cardozo and Rabbi Frances Nataf were very supportive early on. Their input was very helpful. Alan Zaitchik provided excellent comments on several chapters that greatly improved this work. Evan Fales was an unwavering critic, as usual, who forced me to face some difficult issues. I also wish to thank John Kleinig and Tzipporah Kassachkof for their support and appreciated input. Dan Baras read the entire manuscript and made many insightful comments. Finally, Steven Kepnes provided good criticism that I hope I have addressed.

I am blessed to have studied philosophy of religion with Alvin Plantinga, now emeritus from Notre Dame University, USA, and to have learned from him throughout my philosophical career. His combination of deep religious (Christian) commitment and philosophical excellence has been an inspiration to me religiously and philosophically. Also, I am greatly indebted to Rabbi David Hartman for the many years I spent at the Shalom Hartman Institute in Jerusalem and for the many discussions we had on contemporary Judaism and its future.

This project grew out of an invitation by Robert McKim of the University of Illinois at Champaign-Urbana to deliver a lecture in March 2009 on Judaism and world religions. I thank him for the opportunity to have given that lecture and for his philosophical input, and that of his students, which has been most beneficial.

All translations from the Jewish prayer book are quoted with permission of KorenPublishers Jerusalem Ltd. Translation © Jonathan Sacks.

Introduction: With A Wink of the Eye

April 8, 2009. On that day, traditional Jews marked the return of the sun to exactly the place where it was when God popped it into existence 5,769 years ago. They rose early in the morning to pray and to say the blessing they say every 28 years when the sun returns home. I had decided not to participate in this event. I know that the sun was not created 5,769 years ago, and I know that the sun did not pop into existence just like that. The sun is the result of billions of years of gaseous activity, of condensations and explosions. Moreover, God knows that I know this. I can lie to lots of people and fool many people, but there is one person I cannot fool or lie to. That is God. To me, to say the blessing over the return of the prodigal sun would be taking God's name in vain.

Then, as I stood on my Jerusalem porch on the morning of the sun's homecoming, the sun seemed to shine much brighter than usual, as though it knew what was going on down here on earth. As I looked down from my porch to the Jerusalem forest, situated opposite my home, I suddenly saw people, men, women, and children, coming out of the forest, where they had gathered for early morning prayer, returning home after saying the blessing for the sun. They walked silently, deliberately, with an air of majesty and with great dignity. Some of the men were still wearing the *tallit*, the prayer shawl, some of the women carrying their babies. They could have been the Jews walking to the Temple for a holiday celebration in ancient times, or the Jews leaving Spain in a cruel expulsion, or a line of Jews slowly making their way from their ghetto to the train station where cattle cars waited to take them far away. But these were Jews returning from blessing the sun.

Looking down at them, I thought to myself, "I belong with them."

With that, I turned to the sun, shining its holiday face at me, and joined Edie, my wife, in saying the blessing, marking the sun's return to the exact place it was when God popped it into existence 5,769 years ago, just like that.

Then, I winked at God, and God winked at me. And all was well.

I

Setting the Stage

Setting the Stage

The last half-century has seen an important shift in the attitude of the Catholic Church, and of several Protestant churches, toward Judaism and Jews. The landmark event was the proclamation of *Nostra Aetate* on the Church and the Jews, by Pope Paul VI at Vatican II, on October 28, 1965. This document stated that "God holds the Jews most dear," and that "the Jews should not be presented as rejected or accursed by God." Since then, traditional Christian demonizing of Jews and Judaism has been giving way to a more respectful attitude toward Judaism than in the past. Strides have been made in rolling back the age-long teaching of anti-Semitism in Christian Churches. Christian theologians have been creating new, friendly theologies on the Jews and Judaism.

In July 2009, the *Berlin Declaration*, "A Time for Recommitment," issued by the International Council of Christians and Jews, called upon Christians to continue the trajectory of this change. It also called upon Jews to "re-examine Jewish texts and liturgy in the light of these Christian reforms." Jews were to respond in kind to the Christian awakening by scrutinizing their own theologies and liturgies for anti-Christian and anti-Gentile content. What follows here is a positive response by a religious Jew to the call to Jews to re-examine our theology and our attitude toward other religions.

Spinoza pointed out long ago that the Jewish self-identity as God's chosen people has created resentment and enmity toward the Jews for centuries. Particularly, Christianity claimed for its followers the title of "The New People of God," thereby replacing the Jews' claim to the title, which resulted in severe religious competition for the place of honor at

God's table.[1] The Synagogue, so it was said, was blind to the fact that it no longer housed God's chosen people. This attitude is now changing, yet remains a lingering source of inter-religious acrimony.

A task I set myself in this book is to advance mutual religious understanding by presenting a new approach to the doctrine that the Jews are the chosen people, and to follow out the implications of this approach for the relationship between Judaism and other religions.

But this is not the only reason to consider a new theology of the chosen people. The doctrine as previously interpreted has become a stumbling block for many Jews to have a serious engagement with the Jewish religion. They require a revised theology of chosenness to confront the ever-present danger of Jews interpreting the doctrine of chosenness to endorse ethnocentric supremacy, cultural isolation, and the defamation of other religions. Such a rendering of the doctrine in our times signifies not only a combative stance toward other peoples and other religions, but a serious spiritual shortcoming within Judaism itself in the contemporary reality. The need for change is not simply to mollify the Gentiles, but to advance a concept that Jews in general can live by in good conscience in our times. I write from that vantage point for the good of such Jews.

I am not the first Jew to undertake this project. Jewish thinkers before me have written much that is worthwhile and impressive in advancing new ideas on Jewish chosenness.[2] However, I believe that what has gone before is not yet fully adequate to the task. I hope that my proposal will help to advance us toward an acceptable conception of Jewish chosenness for our times.

* * *

That the Jews are God's chosen people is a most distinctive and foundational doctrine of Judaism. Deuteronomy 7:7-8 says:

---

1   For a study of the notion of the Church as "the people of God" in contemporary Catholic theology, see Angela Kim Harkins, "Biblical and Historical Perspectives on 'The People of God,'" in *Transforming Relations: Essays on Jews and Christians throughout History*. In Honor of Michael E. Signer, edited by Franklin T. Harkins (Notre Dame, IN: University of Notre Dame Press, 2010), 319-339.

2   Several of these will be discussed in a later chapter. For a good survey of views of Jewish chosenness, see David Novak, *The Election of Israel: The Idea of the Chosen People* (Cambridge: Cambridge University Press, 1995).

Of all the peoples on earth God chose you to be His treasured people.... Because the LORD loved you, and because He would keep the oath that He swore unto your fathers, has the LORD brought you out with a mighty hand, and redeemed you out of the house of bondage, from the hand of Pharaoh king of Egypt.

Deuteronomy 10:15 declares:

It was to your fathers that the Lord was drawn in His love for them, so that He chose you...

Deuteronomy 14:1-2 states:

You are the children of the LORD your God: you shall not cut yourselves, nor make any baldness between your eyes for the dead. For you are a holy people unto the LORD your God, and the LORD has chosen you to be His own treasure out of all peoples that are upon the face of the earth.

And Amos 3:2 says, "You alone have I known out of all the families of the earth."

The rabbinic literature repeatedly celebrates the Jews as the chosen people, as in this Talmudic passage:

You have made me the sole object of your love,[3] as it is written, Hear Israel, the Lord Our God, The Lord is One. . . (Deuteronomy 6:4)

And I make you the sole object of my love, as it is written, Who is like your people Israel, one nation on earth. (I Chronicles 17:21). (Talmud Hagigah, 3a-3b)

---

3   In translating as "love," I follow the translation of Marcus Jastrow. Rashi's comment would prefer "appreciation" or "praise."

The traditional Jewish prayer book returns again and again to the theme of Jewish chosenness. There is the daily prayer thanking God for having "chosen us" and for giving "us his Torah." In traditional prayer books, a Jew blesses God for not making him or her a Gentile. One prayer thanks God for lovingly "separating" the Jews from the "wayward" nations. The *Aleinu* prayer, appearing in the three daily prayers, declares that God has not, "made us like the nations of the world," and has not made our "lot" like theirs.[4]

You can reform much in Judaism, including Jewish law and at least some Jewish values, and still have yourself a form, however attenuated, of Judaism. However, the concept of Jewish chosenness is too entrenched and ubiquitous in Jewish religious literature to be ignored or excised from a theology of Judaism. In addition, Judaism is a religion of a people, not meant for all of humankind. Without a theology that explains why Judaism is for Jews only (including converts who "become Jews"), Judaism is in danger of becoming a fancy folklore, a vehicle of ethnic identity, or simply what Jews happen to do. As a traditional Jew, I take my religion more seriously than any of those, and so I take Jewish chosenness seriously.

So let me start with a formal definition of what it means to say that the Jews are "*God's chosen people.*" It means that:

1. God has created a permanent, non-revocable relationship with the Jews that God neither has created nor will create with any other nation.

2. This relationship is of supreme value relative to any type of relationship God may have created or will create with any other *specific* nation.

3. The religion of the Jews is integrally related to this special relationship with God.[5]

This is a formal definition that does not say just *what* special relationship exists between God and the Jews that makes the Jews the chosen people. My project in the present work is to present a new understand-

---

4   An additional sentence that has been censored at times goes like this: "For they bow down to naught and emptiness and to a God who does not save." See Chapter Six.
5   The religion is integrally related to the relationship, not just to the belief in the relationship.

ing of the nature of that relationship, and to put forth the possible implications of that understanding for the relationship between Jews and non-Jews and between Judaism and other world religions.

My undertaking this task comes because of my conviction that the Jewish people at large are in need to move beyond extant views on what the relationship *is* between God and the Jews as a nation. My task originated in a dissatisfaction with the implications of at least some of those views for the relationship between Judaism and world religions. Previous understandings may have served well in prior historical circumstances, but require rethinking for the future. My task comes from the conviction that stagnating in old ideas and not going forward with new ones about itself in the world is damaging to Judaism, and also to the Jewish people.

I write from an awareness of trajectories of change that have existed for a long time in Judaism. Theologically, I see these as progressive moments of divine revelation, revelation sometimes bubbling up from the depths of history, rather than descending upon a mountain. Beginning with the Hebrew Bible, in some important areas Judaism has developed over time in the revealing of God's will.[6] (These developments, regrettably, are not necessarily matched by a corresponding direction in individual or collective behavior.) Such developments do not occur in a straight, uninterrupted line, and are not constant. It is more akin to the "punctuated equilibria" of biology, with times of rapid development punctuating relatively long periods of stasis.[7] The history of Judaism is dominated by stasis and by periods of gradual change, but also knows of real change that happens quickly.

Here are two examples, of a great many, of progressive advancement in the revelation of God's will, concerning the Pentateuchal law of the adulterous wife and laws of corporal punishment for causing death, and onward.

In the Semitic Near East of the Pentateuch, waters were often thought to be sacred, embodiments of the gods or infused with the

---

6   After writing these sentences I found almost the same wording in Robert Karl Gnuse, *No Other Gods: Emergent Monotheism in Israel* (Sheffield, England: Sheffield Academic Press, 1997), Chapter 6.

7   The classic paper on punctuated equilibria is N. Eldrege and S. J. Gould, "Punctuated Equilibria: An Alternative to Phyletic Gradualism," in *Models in Paleobiology*, edited by T. J. M. Schopf (San Francisco: Freeman, Cooper, and Co., 1972), 82-115. The application to Israelite religion can be found in Gnuse, *No Other Gods*, Chapter 8.

vital energies of the gods. This gave rise to ordeal by water, typically by casting a suspect of wrongdoing into a river. The sacred river would discern between the pure and the defiled. If the suspect survived, this proved innocence.[8] The Hammurabi Code 132 encodes such an ordeal for a woman suspected of adultery:[9]

> If the "finger is pointed" at a man's wife about another man, but she is not caught sleeping with the other man, she shall jump into the river for her husband.

Jumping into the river refers back to law 2 in the Code to the ordeal by water:

> If any one bring an accusation against a man, and the accused go to the river and leap into the river, if he sink in the river his accuser shall take possession of his house. But if the river prove that the accused is not guilty, and he escape unhurt, then he who had brought the accusation shall be put to death, while he who leaped into the river shall take possession of the house that had belonged to his accuser.

The Hebrew Bible, too, prescribes an ordeal by holy water for a suspected adulterous woman, at Numbers 5. There are important differences between the two legislations, however, differences that show more respect for the woman (relative to the time!) and involve no magical content. The major difference is that the woman drinks the water and is not made to jump into the river. She drinks the water after an elaborate ceremony and an oath. A second difference is that the entire ceremony takes place within the precincts of the Tabernacle. So the holiness of the water is due to its being employed in the holy place of God and the putting of God's name in the water, rather than the water being intrinsically holy. Thirdly, there is no unambiguous indication in the text that the results of the ordeal will be manifest immediately.

---

8   See William Robertson Smith, *Lectures on the Religion of the Semites, The Fundamental Institutions*, Third Edition (New York: Ktav Publishing House, 1969). Chapter 5, especially 179ff.

9   Here and in the next comparison between the Pentateuch and Hammurabi, I do not mean to imply that the relationship is the same regarding all legislative comparisons.

Possibly, the test will be if the woman conceives and has children afterward or will be rendered sterile.[10]

The rabbinical literature further distances the ordeal by water from the broad cultural context and softens the fate of the woman in several ways. The Rabbis moralized the notion of "holy waters." These waters were not intrinsically holy, but became holy when placed in the holy bowl from which the woman drank. And why was the bowl holy? A rabbinical text says that it was holy because it was made from the mirrors that the Israelite women used in Egypt to make themselves attractive to their husbands to insure the continuation of the Israelite nation.[11] The bowl, like the water, has no intrinsic holiness.

In addition, the Rabbis exempted many women from the law of the suspected wife and curtailed its application in many ways. Finally, Rabbi Yochanan ben Zakai abolished the ordeal by water altogether, because adultery was rampant among men, and it was not proper to subject a man's wife to the ordeal when he himself might be adulterous.[12]

Here we see a progressive movement away from the notion of water as intrinsically holy and from the pre-Pentateuchal ceremony.

A second example of progressive reinterpretation is in the law of corporal punishment for murder. The Hammurabi Code, 229, provides for the death penalty for unintentional loss of life:

> If a builder build a house for some one, and does not construct it properly, and the house which he built fall in and kill its owner, then that builder shall be put to death.

In the Torah, in cases of a person causing the death of another, only premeditated murder receives the death penalty. The major view is that an unintentional taking of a life requires exile at a city of refuge, and that no other punishment can be meted out by a court. In addition, unlike in earlier legislation, in the Torah, refuge to a holy site or a sanctuary could not protect a premeditating murderer from arrest and punishment.[13]

---

10 This is argued by Tikva Frymer-Kensky in "The Strange Case of the Suspected Sotah," *Vetus Testamentum*, 34 (1984): 11-26.

11 Bamidbar Rabbah, 9:14

12 *Mishnah, Sotah*, 9:9. This passage might be a post-Mishnaic addition to the tractate. The Talmud (Sotah, 14b) gives as the reason for the abolishment of this law that adultery had become usual with witnesses, and so the law was to be replaced by a straight-out trial for adultery.

13 For an extensive discussion of these laws see Umberto Cassuto, *A Commentary on the Book of*

The rabbinic literature further restricted the application of the death penalty in quite a few ways. Most significant was the saying of the *Mishnah* about the need to restrict the death penalty, and the assertion of Rabbis Akiva and Tarfon in the following passage:

> A Sanhedrin [major court] that executes once in seven years, is called murderous. Rabbi Eliezer b. Azariah Says: once in seventy years. Rabbi Tarfon and Rabbi Akiva say: "Had we been members of a Sanhedrin, no person would ever be put to death. [14]

Judaism also encourages increasing reinterpretation of theological understanding. Traditional Judaism has known many junctures at which there occurred theological reconstructions of some of its fundamental teachings. In the Middle Ages, Maimonides, Gersonides, David Kimchi, and others tried to transform Jewish thinking about God and God's relationship to the world. They saw God in a more abstract way than previously thought, and as far less controlling of the world. In the fourteenth century, Jewish mysticism in the form of *Kabbalah* emerged on the scene, inserting an entirely new vocabulary into Judaism. There was now not only God and the angels, but structures of spiritual worlds and spiritual potencies, *sefirot*. Kabbalists evolved new rituals to manipulate these new entities for the good of the Jewish people and redemption of the world. Later, in the eighteenth century, Hasidism effected a new upheaval in Judaism, in a transformation of values. Prayer was to be the center of the religious life, not Torah study. The saintly *zaddik* could raise his followers to God through his efforts on their behalf; and, at times, duties of the heart were to trump duties of the body.

In sum, we find slow, piecemeal developments in new directions in

---

Exodus (Jerusalem: Magnes Publishing House, 1967), 265ff.

14   Mishnah, Makot 1:10. However, Rabbi Shim'on ben Gamliel replies that if so, these two would have caused an increase in murders in Israel. Another instructive example pertains to a minor daughter. The Mishnah decrees that a father has complete control over his minor daughter, and, in keeping with Scriptures, he can sell her as a slave or transfer her in marriage without her consent. This legislation is actually an advance on the custom of female infanticide that was prevalent in Greek and Roman culture. Infanticide is not tolerated in Jewish law. Mark Golden estimates that in ancient Athens the female infanticide rate was twenty percent. (Mark Golden, "Demography and the Exposure of Girls at Athens," *Phoenix* 35 (1981): 316-331, as quoted by Sarah B. Pomeroy, *Spartan Women* (Oxford: Oxford University, 2002), 35.)

various areas of Jewish law. And newer, more sophisticated understand-ings of God have arisen. In the evolving of this trajectory, there is no sharp distinction between what God reveals and what humans realize. God's voice at Sinai continues to be heard and continues to prod us to ever more refined understandings of God's word. As the Rabbis said, "Every day shall they be new in your eyes, as though this very day you received them from Sinai" (*Psikta Zutrata Deuteronomy*, Vaetchanan). On my understanding, progressive revelation is an historical process that beats within the rhythms of human history. The new comes to light when the proper vessels for holding it have evolved, and not before.

Some, no doubt, will view these historical changes simply as succes-sive rejections of what went before, and no more. But it is also possible to see these changes as a revelational process, one in which core mean-ings are raised up from within coverings that were needed in their times and which hid the emerging understandings. My aim is to contribute somewhat to advancing discussion in the ongoing process of coming closer to understanding God's will for the Jewish people.

In what follows, I will present a theological revision for our times of the notion that the Jews are God's chosen people, and I will undertake a correlative reinterpretation of some traditional texts. My view repre-sents new values and new insights that are coming into reality in our contemporary world, through God's grace. Old conceptions of the Jews as God's chosen people might have served the purposes of history at various times, but now it is time to continue the trajectory of Judaism into the future. The idea I present in this study, if accepted and developed further by others—surely with modifications and improvements—will have waited for this time in history to become a collectively formulated and accepted understanding of God's teaching for us.

* * *

I will be focusing on the idea of the chosenness of the Jews, and then, once I have explored this idea, I will draw the implications for how Judaism should relate to religious diversity. In treating the "chosen people" theme, however, I will not be trying to explain why God chose *specifically* the Jewish people, rather than, say, the Hittites. Instead, I will be offering an explanation why *any* chosen people might exist in God's world, whether that people be the Jews *or* the Hittites. On my explanation, it will turn out that it was a good and proper thing for God to have chosen *a* people to be God's chosen people.

In what follows, I will be writing from within traditional Judaism. My theories assume that a core of traditional Judaism is true; at the very least that there is a God, and that God chose the Jewish people. Yet, the stance I take is what I would call that of a *critical traditionalist*. By calling myself a *traditionalist* I mean that my view retains central elements of traditional Judaism, and also that I make use of traditional Judaic sources. By calling myself a *critical* traditionalist, on the other hand, I mean to say that I am supplementing previous conceptions of chosenness that I find in Judaism. Furthermore, my stance is critical in that I make no claim to authority when using traditional texts, and no claim to historical correctness about what "Judaism teaches" or has taught. This is my own view. And it is a view for the future. I provide a program to be implemented to think of Jewish chosenness in a new way. I do not speak in the name of Rabbis or of any Jewish philosophers. My use of traditional texts has the purpose of having a view that grows *out* of the tradition, picking up on strands in the rich history of Judaic thought.

In particular, I will be employing rabbinic texts to shape my view of Jewish chosenness. My use of those texts is selective. Indeed, many other such texts clash with ones I carefully choose. In being selective, I embrace an important tradition in Judaism regarding the authority, or lack of it, of the non-legal rabbinic literature, the *aggadah*. Historically, many important Jewish rabbis declared that the *aggadah* literature was not binding, in the sense that a Jew was not obligated to believe its truth. Saadia Gaon (882-942), Samuel ben Hofni (d. 1034), Sherira Gaon (906-1066), Hai Gaon (939-1038), Abraham Ibn Ezra (1092-1167), Maimonides (1138–1204), Abraham son of Maimonides (1186-1237), David Kimchi (1160-1235), and others held this view of the *aggadah*. The aggadic literature expressed the views of various Rabbis facing their times and their constituencies, but does not have binding force beyond then and there.

To me, the *aggadah* literature deserves the greatest respect and serves as the rock upon which Jewish thought is to proceed. If we are as humans, the rabbis of the *aggadah* were as angels. However, in times such as ours, that bring such a radical departure from the past, we must look beyond the great ones who composed the rabbinic literature and see what they could not have imagined. The Rabbis are the starting point, always to be taken into account, never ignored. But they cannot be the end point. In what follows I walk a thin line between loyalty to the community of traditional Jews and an independence of thought and action that diverges from what that community might deem normative.

In what follows I will be displaying my vision of Jewish chosenness for the future, and explaining how I got to that vision. My hope is that readers who share my general philosophical orientation of critical traditionalism will find here an attractive view that they can either adopt for their own or that they can develop and improve on for their own theology of chosenness. I have also in mind readers who might not share my general orientation but who will be impressed by my vision sufficiently to reconsider their outlook and find a way forward for them. I have little to say directly to someone who is adamantly against my approach to Judaism, and is satisfied with one of the presently normative views about Jewish chosenness and religious diversity. Being myself a person who at one time would have rejected the approach of this book, I can hope that the time will come when they will see things differently.

I turn now to a number of issues that will help set a framework for the ensuing discussions.

God and Biblical Events

In this work I will be talking a lot about God: God's choosing the Jews, what God wants for the Jewish people, for humanity, and how God goes about getting to God's goals. This is meant to be constructive theology and not prophecy or crystal ball reading. Constructive theology tries to make the best sense of the religious tradition in light of deepening spiritual sensibilities, our contemporary scientific knowledge, and acceptable contemporary values. Before going in to my project of constructive theology I want to explain something about my concept of God. Also, in what follows I will be referring often to and making much of biblical events: the Exodus from Egypt, the revelation at Mt. Sinai, and further events from the Hebrew Bible. Some readers might doubt the historicity of these events, or doubt at least the extent of their historicity. For those who are theologically inclined but skeptical about history, I want to offer a way for them to stay with me in what follows.

God

I take discourse about God to be intended to be objective, intended to be about a reality that actually exists and has features of its own, independently of how anybody thinks of it. My view of God, then, is what philosophers call a "realist" one. So I am rejecting, for example, an analysis of discourse about God that sees it as an imaginative fiction designed to express or encourage a commitment to a way of life. So, to say "God chose the Jews" is not, for example, a way of trying to inspire Jews to do good deeds or to contribute money to worthy Jewish causes. It makes a statement that is meant to be true. Neither is talk about God merely "symbolic," meant to point out certain features of natural reality. And "God" is not only a "regulative concept" to guide our lives.

Now, on the one hand, I do not take God to be very much like human beings. With regard to almost everything said about God, I do not take them as having literal meaning. So when I say, "God has chosen the Jews," I do not imagine God mulling things over and then making a decision to choose the Jews. And if I say, "God loves all of humankind equally," I do not see God's love as involving precisely the kinds of emotions humans have when feeling love. God is covered in mystery. "Clouds and darkness surround Him" (Psalms 97:2). I do not believe that any human knows much about what God is really like, or what in our language corresponds to what God is really like. On the other hand, while I acknowledge that God is covered in mystery, I do not suffer from what William Alston once called "transcendentitis," which is the condition of people who maintain that God is absolutely unknowable (at least by any positive predicate).[15] This condition does not do justice to the nature of the religious life, and too often is the last safe-house for those who find it difficult to believe in God at all. My view of God finds a middle path between literalism and transcendentitis.

Consider the relationship between a computer's chip and hard-disk (the "inside"), on the one hand, and what you see on the screen when you view the computer, on the other: (1) What you see on the screen is the result of what is inscribed in the inside. Change the contents in the inside and you will get something different showing on the screen.

---

15 Alston wrote, "I fear that much of twentieth century theology is affected by what we might call 'transcendentitis.'" In, William P. Alston, "Realism and the Christian Faith," *International Journal for Philosophy of Religion*, 38 (1995): 37-60.

(2) What is inscribed in the inside is nothing like what you get on the screen. Inscribed in the inside are no colors or shapes of the picture on the screen. You can peer into the inside in the most powerful microscope and you will see no pictures of people or words. (3) The computer has a translation mechanism that accounts for what you see on the screen as being a *correct* expression of what is inscribed in the inside. (4) What comes on the screen can be distorted by factors neither inscribed in the inside nor due to the translation mechanism from inside to screen, such as electrical interference or dirt on the screen. Even then, there is a rout from the inside to the screen that projects correctly from the inside to the screen.

My way between literalism and transcendentitis concerning God uses this analogy. (1) The way God is perceived in the world is the result of God's very self (the "inside"). Had God been different, then the world would have had a different perception of God. (2) In God there is nothing like what you get on the world-screen. If we knew God as God is, we would not see what we see when we see God on the world-screen. (3) There exists a metaphysical mechanism responsible for the correct projection into the world of what is in God. (4) What comes on the world-screen can be distorted by factors outside the mechanism, such as by psychological interference or by "pollution" on the world-screen. Even then, there is a route from God to the world-screen that projects *correctly* from God to the world-screen.

So, (1) To say that God chose the Jews is to refer to something that really is in God. (2) What really is in God is nothing like what we can imagine as God's choosing the Jews, (3) When we say that God chose the Jews we are reporting the way in which God's self is correctly projected into our understanding. What we say is the correct way for us to think about God, given the mechanism tying what we say to what the true nature of God is. (4) The way we receive the projection can be distorted by factors not included in the correct projection of the idea of God choosing the Jews.

So, on my theology to say, for example, that God is a person, is to say something like this: "There is something in God that is projected into the world correctly as God's personality, but in God there is no personality." And to say, "God has chosen the Jews," is to say that there is something in God correctly projected into the world as God's choosing the Jews, but in God there is nothing to be so identified. The projections are correct, and nearly all of us can do no better than to relate to God as we perceive the projection.

God, on my theology, intends for the projection to be adequate, for practical purposes, to the nature of God's self. This translates into saying roughly that the mechanism of projection is itself grounded in God. In addition, the projection of God into the world serves as a starting point for moving to greater understanding of God beyond the projection. Here enters the distinction between exoteric and esoteric understandings of God. The "exoteric" corresponds to the level at which the world perceives the projection of God. The "esoteric" begins with the realization that the projection, while "correct," does not correspond to what is in God, and continues into deeper levels of finding out what God is in God's self. [16] At the esoteric level, such statements as "God chose the Jews" might receive a new interpretation, isomorphic to its plain meaning or drop away in favor of a statement closer to the truth of the matter.

There are two points of disanalogy in my analogy between God and the internal realm of a computer. The first is this: Whereas the contents and make-up of the computer's inside is commonly known to humanity, what is in God is rarely known by a human being, and even then only partially and haltingly. And when a human being does gain some insight into what is in the God-inside, it may be so unlike what is projected into the world that she has few, if any, words to describe it directly. It is from the perception of these human beings, among other things, that we know about the very existence of the God-inside in the first place.

The second point of disanalogy is that, unlike with the computer screen, God is projected onto the world in different ways both in different eras as well as during a single time period. The idea of God has changed over time and continues to do so before our very eyes. (Consider process theology and feminist conceptions of God.[17]) It would take me too far afield from my specific task in this book to attempt a really adequate

---

16 For a good exposition of the distinction between exoteric and esoteric conceptions of God in Western religions, see Frithjof Schuon, *The Transcendent Unity of Religions* (Wheaten, IL: Theosophical Publishing House, 1984), especially Chapters 1-3. Schuon believes in a commonality of all Western religions at the esoteric level.

17 For the concept of God in Jewish process theology, see: William E. Kaufman, *The Evolving God in Jewish Process Theology* (Lewiston, NY: Edwin Mellen Press, 1997). For a classic statement of a Jewish feminist concept of God, see: Judith Plaskow, *Standing Again at Sinai: Judaism from a Feminist Perspective* (San Francisco: Harper Collins, 1991), Chapter 4.

theology of this fact. My view of the Jews as the chosen people, however, will carry with it some thoughts on the multiplicity of God-ideas in world history.

Now, in order to follow me forward you need not accept my concept of God. In fact you need not believe in God at all. You could be what Andrew Eshleman calls a "fictionalist" about God. Fictionalists, for Eshleman, do not believe in God, yet: "they hold that it is reasonable for an atheist to pursue a form of life shaped by full engagement with theistic religious language and practice...by reinterpreting religious language and belief in a non-realist manner."[18] They might do so because they take a religious tradition to embody an ideal to be lived for not fully expressible or pursuable in a secular way.[19] Fictionalists are "religious" in the sense of locating themselves within a religious community they define by: "We are the people who are committed to doing X and aspire to Y," rather than "We are the people who believe these propositions about God.[20]

You might even be an "incipient fictionalist," one who does not believe that God exists, but who would like to adopt Judaism as your own because you find yourself attracted to "doing X and aspiring to Y" in the way Judaism does. Yet you might have reservations about some of the ideals, including those accompanying extant versions of the Jews as God's chosen people. If so, I hope that my proposal for Jewish chosenness will help you become at least a full fictionalist, if I cannot convince you of more. Incipient fictionalists are invited to come along as well.

Biblical Narratives

Suppose you have doubts about the historical reliability of the stories about Abraham, the Exodus, the Siniatic revelation, or the like. You will then likely be put off by my references to these events as though they actually occurred, and occurred the way the Bible presents them. But you might be open to a theological understanding of the Bible nonethe-

---

18 Andrew S. Eshleman, "Can an Atheist Believe in God?" *Religious Studies* 41 (2005): 184. For a Jewish view that comes close to fictionalism, see Tamar Ross, *Expanding the Palace of Torah: Orthodoxy and Feminism* (Waltham, MA: Brandeis University Press, 2004), Chapter 10.

19 Andrew S. Eshleman, "Religious Fictionalism Defended: Reply to Cordy," *Religious Studies* 46 (2010): 96.

20 Eshleman, "Religious Fictionalism," 95.

less. So here I want to try to convince you to stick around by explaining the minimal system requirements you will need to do so. And they do not include accepting the Hebrew Bible as Gospel truth.

To be open to the way my view of Jewish chosenness invokes biblical events, it will be sufficient to accept as a minimum the following two positions:

First, assume that the Hebrew Bible represents a combination of actual memories of past events and a selective reshaping of those memories. Mark Smith, for example, has argued this extensively.[21] This means that the Hebrew Bible reflects a time later than the remembered, recorded events, with a mature monotheistic understanding that developed over time. And the Hebrew Bible reflects a later sense of how God is related to the Israelites. This sense was continued when the Israelites became known as the "Jews." It is not the actual occurrence of the biblical events that is crucial, but what is reflected in those stories of memory and historical reconstruction.[22]

Secondly, the explanation for how the recording of biblical stories and concomitant conceptions developed the way they did is not to be exclusively in terms of socio-political developments. Rather, socio-political explanations are to be supplemented in at least two ways. To start with, we are to allow that at a very high level of explanation, divine activity was shaping at least some socio-political events, in some manner, so as to fulfill divine purposes. This need not imply a broad, tight control of history by God, only a subtle general directing for a divine purpose, something like how a complex and diverse process receives its overall shape from the shape of the vessel in which it takes place. Also, socio-political explanations will be supplemented by explanations in terms of a religious impulse, representing various stages of response to an awareness of God, whether conscious or subliminal. Religious consciousness is to be taken to be as least as basic to human flourishing as are social, political, and economic concerns.

Here is an example of what I am after. Mark Smith argues that Israelite monotheism developed around the eighth century BCE. It came, according to Smith, in place of a conception of Israelite divinity

---

21 Mark S. Smith, *The Memoirs of God: History, Memory, and the Experience of God in Ancient Israel* (Minneapolis: Fortress Press, 2004).

22 For a study of memory vs. historiography in Judaism see Yosef Hayim Yerushalmi, *Zakhor: Jewish History and Jewish Memory* (Seattle and London: University of Washington Press, 1982).

that thought in terms of a family of gods. Now, Smith explains this change as due entirely, it seems, to the alleged lowered value of the human family in the eighth century BCE, and the rise of the importance of the individual person. Just so, the one God as an individual came to replace the family of gods.

This purely naturalistic explanation of the emergence of monotheism among the ancient Israelites requires supplementation in the ways I have described in the above paragraph. Theologically, religious impulses are to be included as *sui generis* factors in such developments, and further down the road I would want to ground those impulses in Divine activity behind the scenes. Many questions remain as to the relationship between religious and naturalistic explanations, but I will not enter further into this topic here.

So, if you do not accept the historicity of the Exodus, for example, you can employ a translation scheme for such statements as, "God took the Israelites out of Egypt" to get something like this: "When the Hebrew Bible was formed, the story of the Exodus was expressive of the Israelite consciousness of God at that time, and that consciousness remained thereafter." And I would urge you to add, "And this consciousness was advanced by the actual relationship of the people to God."[23]

An Objection—Human Values

Some readers might think that my project is illicit, wrongheaded, and should not be pursued due to the kind of protest once lodged by Michael Wyschogrod. Wyschogrod wrote that

> much of religious apology limits God's sovereignty as it proves that he could not have done anything other than he did, or . . . that what he did measures up to the highest standards of morality. . . . The apologist does not realize that he has subjected God to judgment by criteria other than his free and sovereign will . . . and is therefore no longer talking of the biblical God. We must avoid this

---

23 In Chapter Six, in connection with the conquest narratives I will be advancing a further way of avoiding commitment to historical narratives and retaining the force of my presentation. I refer to allegorical interpretation.

sort of justification at all cost. . . .[24]

I plead guilty to the charge of making the idea of God's choosing the Jews meet the highest standards of morality, but reject the claim that this is to be avoided at all costs. On the contrary. While there is place in the religious life for a person to defer to God's sovereignty, and even to bow to God's inscrutability, that can be expected of a person only if she is either a dogmatic "true believer" or has sufficient reason to believe in and trust a sovereign or inscrutable God. My project does not speak to dogmatic true believers. As for the others, many of us will withhold our deference to God's sovereignty until we are convinced that, at the core, God is morally upright and does not act capriciously. Only then can you ask of us to trust God in those situations in which God appears to act in ways mysterious and beyond our moral understanding. If the result is not the God of the Bible, as Wyschogrod maintains, that will be because most of us today are not the *people* in the Bible. We look at God through prisms of both tradition and modernity, and must make do with what we are. For this reason I must reject this type of objection to finding a new conception of the Jews as God's chosen people because of contemporary values.

At the same time, there is an important warning in Wyschogrod's words. We must be moderate in what we *think* is morally correct, being open to the possibility of being wrong. However, as I have said, we have no choice but to employ our moral sensibilities if we are to gain confidence in God for those situations in which God's behavior is morally inscrutable. In addition, I see, cautiously, evolving moral sensibilities as a type of revelation bubbling up from the depths of history. Our values of today might yet be superseded by others. Yet, at any one stage of moral development we have no alternative but to adjust our theologies.

Another Objection—The Shoah

My view of Jewish chosenness includes that God has an ongoing great love for the Jewish people, a love that continues to figure in the history of the people to the present time. The massive destruction of European (and

---

24   Michael Wyschogrod, *The Body of Faith: Judaism as Corporeal Election* (Minneapolis: Seabury Press, 1983), 58.

some non-European) Jews leading up to and during the Second World War contests this contention strongly. Millions of Jews were murdered, tortured, and agonizingly brutalized over a period of many years. Those who survived were marked with scars far deeper than the heart can reach. The suffering of surviving parents has in many cases been handed down to the second generation and even to the third. The destruction, dislocation, and desolation of the Jewish people in the European Destruction constitute a devastating attack on the very idea that God's love of the Jewish people has expression in history, and continues through and after the European Destruction. As Rabbi Irving Greenberg has eloquently declared, "No statement, theological or otherwise, should be made that would not be credible in the presence of burning children."[25] Can a concept of Jewish chosenness involving God's ongoing great love for the Jews in history be at all credible in the face of such a challenge?

Various theologies have appeared in response to the European Destruction, including that God is far from perfect, that God hid his face, that God withdrew from history, and that God violated the covenant and so as a result Jews are no longer bound by it.[26] I do not subscribe to any of these theological understandings any more than I accept that the Shoah was punishment for the sins of the Jews, or that it was part of God's plan to lead to the creation of the country of Israel and a new era in Jewish history.

I reject all of these from the conviction that no theology can properly respond to the Destruction. That is because the Destruction was too enormous, too grotesque, too searing, too full of human misery, to be understood theologically as an event *within history*. No. The Shoah was a *rupture* in history, a puncture in history. History was put aside as we plunged into a black hole that lets out no light. The Shoah is incommensurate with history. No attempt to place it into history will succeed. It itself belongs elsewhere, outside.

This is why I am so moved by a response to the suffering in the Warsaw Ghetto by Rabbi Klonymous Kalman Shapiro, the Piececzner Rebbe. The Rebbe sees the suffering, children being shot in the streets

---

25 Irving Greenberg, "Cloud of Smoke, Pillar of Fire: Judaism, Christianity, and Modernity after the Holocaust," in *Auschwitz: Beginning of a New Era?*, edited by E. Fleischner (New York: Ktav Publishing House, 1977), 23.

26 For an excellent collection on the subject see Steven T. Katz, ed., *The Impact of the Holocaust on Jewish Theology* (New York and London: New York University Press, 2005).

just for fun by passing Nazis, and children dying from hunger on the ghetto sidewalks. He understands that there can be no explanation of this in terms of God's having decided to behave in a certain way towards God's people. He has no recourse but to theorize that what is going on cannot be anything less than a catastrophic upheaval *within the very being of God itself*, a cosmic earthquake taking place in the ground of all being. It must be that God is being shaken up in the innermost places. God must be enduring great suffering by forces deep in God's very being. And the Jews, yes, the Jews, God's chosen people, are the locus in God's creation where the Divine suffering breaks out and goes beyond human endurance. The Shoah is a reverberation of God's suffering in creation, Jewish suffering configuring the catastrophic upheaval in God, taking place outside of history.

Now, I do not mean to endorse this as "the explanation" of the European Destruction. What happens within the being of God is beyond our ken. (Neither am I sure that I accept the implications of the nature of the Jews' relationship to God implied by the Rebbe.) Further, I would not want to exonerate the Nazis of their deeds on the grounds that the events came from within God's very being. (Neither would the Rebbe). However, what does strike me as right in this is the refusal to place the Shoah within the historical behavior of God toward the chosen people. It is too enormous for that.

So, I conclude that *theologically* we must pass over the European Destruction in silence. But even that is not quite right: for we must not even be silent. We must continue as before and not allow the Shoah to be demoted to being a part of history. We cannot proceed theologically quite exactly as before, however, since our confidence must be shaken in the validity of our theologizing. Aware that catastrophic ruptures can and do occur in history, we must be many-fold diligent to maintain modesty and openness. I accept that obligation on myself.

Finally, we should be on guard against gauging one's identification with the Shoah by how angry one is with God, or by how much one demands a change in our attitude toward God. My theological position is not only compatible with the deepest sympathy for the victims and survivors of the Destruction, but is a result of that sympathy to the greatest degree to which I am capable.

So, I will carry on with my affirmation of God's continuing great love of the Jewish people.

* * *

I now turn to a review of the chapters of this book. I begin my project in the next chapter, "Choosing Chosenness," with the criteria I employ in arriving at my own view of Jewish chosenness. I will be explaining these criteria and will explain how I got to these conditions of acceptability for a contemporary view of chosenness.

In defending criteria of any sort, one meets up with what Roderick Chisholm called the "problem of criteria," namely that one will have to have criteria for choosing *those* criteria.[27] But then, one will need criteria for choosing just those criteria that one used to choose the original criteria. And so forth. The point is that the justification of criteria must start from somewhere without further justification. Some of my criteria are rock-bottom of my commitments. They serve to justify other things I believe in and to which I am committed. There exists nothing deeper in me from which their justification comes. For that reason, there is not that much I can say to back up some of my criteria with reasons that will be more deeply embedded in my scheme of justification. So, I will explain how I came to hold these criteria and illustrate how they function in my life, and hope that the reader will be moved to consider my criteria for his or her own.

In Chapter Three, "Views of Chosenness," I survey a number of important extant views of chosenness to decide what I find acceptable in them and what begs for replacement or supplementation. These include views coming from interpretations of biblical verses, rabbinic literature, medieval Jewish philosophy, the *kabbalah*, modern Jewish thought, and contemporary thinkers. The best of them, I argue, require supplementation before they are acceptable.

In Chapter Four, "For God's Love has Overwhelmed Us," I present my own view of Jewish chosenness. According to my view of chosen peoplehood, God loves all peoples equally. God does not love the Jews more than any other nation. My presentation will start with some thoughts of Søren Kierkegaard on Christian incarnational theology and with related thoughts of several other Christian philosophers, as well as Jewish

---

27 Roderick M. Chisholm, *The Foundations of Knowing* (Minneapolis: University of Minnesota Press, 1982), 62ff.

sources. I will utilize these insights in building my conception of Jewish chosenness. Following that, I will present in Chapter Five a new conception of a Jewish relationship to other world religions. I defend a new Jewish approach to dialogue between Judaism and other religions to the advantage of both, without risking compromise on theological honesty.

Chapter Six, "Reinterpreting Tradition," first defends against some anticipated objections to my proposal and then is a constructive attempt to apply my view to selections of the Hebrew Bible and Jewish liturgy. I will be offering re-interpretations of several of these texts as well as new directions in prayer, given my approach to Jewish chosenness. My purpose will be to expand my understanding of chosenness and show its viability in the religious life of a Jew. I round out this chapter with a summary and a look at the future of the chosen people in the country of Israel.

That is my book on one leg. As for the rest, "Go read it!"

II

Choosing Chosenness: Criteria

In this chapter, I present my criteria for the acceptability of any contemporary view of Jewish chosenness. In the following chapter, I will use these criteria to explain what I accept and do not accept in other selected conceptions of chosenness. Hopefully, this will prepare you for Chapter Four, in which I propose my own view of Jewish chosenness.

A view of chosenness and Judaism is acceptable to me only if it meets these criteria:

1. It is compatible with Judaic religious *open exclusivism.*

2. It advances a respectful and appreciative attitude, *in principle*, toward other world religions.[1]

3. It does not imply Jewish superiority or imply a degradation of non-Jews.

4. It has our relationship with God at its center.

5. It makes use of traditional Jewish sources.

6. It has plausibility, granting a critically traditional Judaic perspective, in light of what we know of the contemporary world and what we can hope for in the future.

Here follows an elaboration of each of these criteria.

Criterion A

The term "religious open exclusivism" in criterion A is a technical one.[2] Beginning with "exclusivism," I am interested here in *truth-exclusivism,*

---

1   I say "in principle," because any religion might make mistakes. I reserve the right to reject elements of religions that are obviously immoral or obviously in conflict with the facts, as we know them. More on this below.

2   See Jonathan L. Kvanvig, "Religious Pluralism and the Buridan's Ass Paradox," *European Journal for Philosophy of Religion*, 1 (2009): 1-26, for a use of such terminology.

that is, exclusivism about truth.[3] I am an "open exclusivist" about religious truth. A person is *truth-exclusivist* about a religion when maintaining that it has core teachings all of which are true and also maintains that all other religions have at least one false core belief.[4] It is *exclusivist* in the sense of *excluding* all other religions from having *all* true core beliefs.[5] Notice that being a truth-exclusivist about one's religion is consistent with believing that religion to teach some false beliefs, as long as the latter are not considered *core* beliefs. Also notice that there need be no general agreement among devotees of a given religion as to what *are* the core beliefs of that religion, nor about what are the core beliefs of a different religion. A person is an exclusivist relative to the core beliefs that person countenances as such. In addition, over time a person might shift judgment as to just which teachings of the home religion or another religion *are* core ones, thereby preserving an exclusivist perspective in the face of newly acknowledged false beliefs in the home religion.

My exclusivism is an "open" one, by which I mean that it is open to religions other than Judaism containing truths not found in Judaism, or far less accessible there, that it would be most worthwhile for Jews to know about, ponder, and maybe even accept. And it is open to religions other than Judaism having content that drives home shared truths in an especially poignant and impressive way. Religions other than Judaism could contain stories, allegories, teachings, and practices that give a cognitive or emotional wallop to things that Judaism itself teaches. Finally, I am open to other religions having practices that Judaism does not have, which can enhance the spiritual goals of my religion. This can include some forms of meditative prayer, for example, not found in Judaism. In short, my exclusivism is open to the real possibility that the

---

3   Some other forms of exclusivism would be ritual exclusivism, salvific exclusivism, value exclusivism, and revelational exclusivism.

4   My formulation fails to cover the case where the core beliefs of a foreign religion are a proper subset of those of the home religion. In that case, the home religion can deem true all the core beliefs of the foreign religion, since they are all identical with truths in the home religion. Such might be the relationship, roughly, between Mormonism and some standard forms of Christianity. A full formulation of exclusivism would include a rejection of the aforesaid foreign sub-set religion as incomplete, truth-inadequate. Since such a stance does not appear among the extant major religions, I omit it from the discussion.

5   A more robust definition of religious truth-exclusivism would relate to degrees of success in truth beyond core beliefs. I ignore that component here because of various complexities arising in the formulation, complexities not relevant to us here. For a thorough presentation of definitions of religious exclusivism, see Robert McKim, *On Religious Diversity* (Oxford: Oxford University Press, 2012).

accumulated wisdom of other world religions can enhance and enrich my own Jewish spiritual life. My openness to other religions has taught me that all of the possibilities I have mentioned here are indeed actual at some point or another.[6]

In endorsing exclusivism in my criterion A, I mean to reject a number of views. These are: (1) that there is no "truth" in religion, (2) that truth does not matter in religion, (3) that all religions are "equally true" or "equally false," and (4) that talk about Jewish chosenness is simply an internal Jewish discourse with no implications beyond itself, and really is not to be taken all that seriously.

I am old-fashioned about truth in religion and in general. No fancy post-modernism for me, which denounces truth as a cover for coercive political and social abuse and eschews truth in favor of "human-constructs." I believe the post-modernist program to be redeeming of many social ills. However, along with some important philosophers, such as Alvin Goldman and Alvin Plantinga, I think post-modernism is hopelessly incoherent when it comes to its doctrine of truth.[7]

When speaking of truth, I do not speak metaphorically or picturesquely. I use the word "truth" in a straightforward, old-fashioned sense. You and I don't have to agree on what *is* true in order for you to agree with me *about* truth. You can accept my view on truth while we argue for seven days and seven nights about what *is* true.

The above pertains to the metaphysics of truth, the kind of thing truth is. *Asserting* truth is a different matter. I allow asserting truth, and even being rather dogmatic about it, only *for all practical purposes.* We must be conscious always of the fact that our finite vision might not be correct. But we have no choice but to do the best we can.

Please, do not close this book because you don't agree with me about truth, or because you cannot agree with me in rejecting the above four views about truth and religion. You might still find that my view of Jewish chosenness appeals to you more than any others, in any case, and so be willing to consider it for your own. The present criterion is a

---

6   Some would consider my stance a type of "pluralism," I avoid that term here because of its association with views that deny that one religion has more core truths than another. I am not a pluralist in that sense.

7   Alvin Goldman, *Knowledge in a Social World* (Oxford: Oxford University, 1999), and Alvin Plantinga, "Postmodernism and Pluralism," in *Warranted Christian Belief* (Oxford: Oxford University Press, 2000), 422-457.

necessary condition of *my* accepting a view of chosenness, and I know that it is a condition for many other people as well. If I can make out a satisfactory notion of chosenness consistent with my idea of truth, it should surely work for other ideas of truth. In any case, you might agree with my view on chosenness without accepting all of my criteria.

What I am saying about Judaism is not to be confused with the claim that *everything* in Judaism is true. I speak of a core of truth. I am, after all, a *critical* traditionalist. Among the core truths of Judaism, I include, among others, the truth that God exists, as well as, yes, that the Jews are God's chosen people, however these truths are going to be explicated in detail. And when I say that these things are "true" I mean that in the same sense of "true" that one might say that it is true that there are mountains and electrons, and it is true that George Washington was the first president of the United States. Of course, that God exists or that God chose the Jews is not an empirical claim attested to by the senses. But the sense of "true" is the same throughout. There are different kinds of truths only in the same sense as there are different kinds of people. In both cases, "truth" and "person" retain a uniform meaning.

Finally, I do not subscribe to what has become a lasting legacy of the Enlightenment: permitting saying something is true (or, that it is "rational" to believe something) only if it can be "proven" by sense-experience and scientific investigation. The adoption of this dogma was a political-social move in history in which some people got together and said to each other: "Look, let's avoid religious wars and a lot of acrimony and silliness, by limiting everyone to stuff that we can enforce general agreement over. So let's restrict people's minds to sense-evidence and scientific conclusions. And let's enforce this by making everything else irrational or at best a-rational." This proposal seemed quite promising following the Thirty Years War (1618-1648), in which most of Western Europe waged battles, predominantly between Catholics and Protestants. The old order of Christendom had collapsed and something had to be done to restore order.

I find this proposal to be non-compelling. It makes it impossible to reach truths that might be out there beyond the reach of science and sense perception. A person is entitled to look at all the evidence available to her and make the best judgment of how it all makes sense. Surely, this can be influenced by one's background and by unrecognized biases. But that is the human condition, and we must live and make judgments on what we have to go on. This is what a behaviorist does when she becomes convinced that behaviorism is the best way to understand human psychology. And this is what an existentialist therapist does when he thinks otherwise. Given the human need to make judgments to shape our lives, the Enlightenment program was doomed from the start.

In any event, I side with William James in his reply to William Clifford. Clifford had stated that "It is wrong always, everywhere, and for anyone, to believe anything upon insufficient evidence," where "evidence" was to be only in the scientific sense.[8] James argued, against Clifford, that the risk of holding false beliefs was far outweighed by the risk of losing the possibility of gaining true beliefs.[9]

In order to prevent religious wars, we do not have to forbid people from holding religious exclusivist beliefs. Instead, we have to cultivate a civil culture of dissent and disagreement, and work for the obtaining of openness to go along with exclusivism. If a person holds exclusivist religious truths it does not have to lead inevitably to wars, violence, or intolerance, any more than being a loyal fan of a football team *must* lead to stadium violence. (Unless, of course, these beliefs include things like, "Kill all believers in other religions," or the like.) Much progress remains in moderating religious violence and intolerance, but what lies ahead should not be a prohibition on religious truth.

So, my criterion A commits me to core truths in Judaism and to rejecting as false the beliefs of other religions that contradict those core truths. And the chosenness of the Jews is my relevant core-truth here. You can fool around with Jewish law to update it to contemporary times. You can pick and choose which values of Jewish tradition you will emphasize and which you will allow to recede to the background. You can abolish all differences between men and women in Judaism. In all these cases you might still end up with a form of traditional Judaism, if only by a stretch. However, do away with Jewish chosenness, *in every sense,* as true, and you abandon traditional Judaism as well.

The chosenness of the Jewish people is so woven into the fabric of the religion that Judaism as an historical religion would not be recog-

---

8   Clifford's dictum appears in "The Ethics of Belief," in William Clifford, *Lectures and Essays,* edited by Leslie Stephen and Frederick Pollock (London: Macmillan, 1879).

9   William James, "The Will to Believe," in William James, *The Will to Believe and Other Essays in Popular Philosophy, and Human Immortality* (New York: Dover Publications, 1956).

nizable without it. The biblical stories, the narratives of history, and the liturgy would no longer be familiar were you to delete this theme.[10] As the Christian theologian, Hans Kung, writes of the doctrine of the Jews as God's Chosen People, "Specific references are superfluous for an idea which runs through the whole Old Testament."[11] To fulfill my criterion A, you have to provide some worthwhile sense of Jewish chosenness.

My purpose in what follows is to show that a contemporary doctrine of the Jews as God's chosen people is forthcoming even if one takes an exclusivist view of Judaism (albeit an open exclusivist view). Were I to take a weaker position on truth, such as that all religions have equal "validity," my task would be easier.[12] However, not only do I not personally endorse that view, but a great many traditional Jews do not endorse it either. A feature of my proposal about Jewish chosenness is that one may be an exclusivist about Judaism and at the same time adopt a contemporary advance on the ancient doctrine of the Jews being God's chosen people.

Criterion B

Criterion B is a corollary of the "open" part of my open exclusivism in A. B calls for a respectful and appreciative attitude, *in principle*, toward other world religions. Traditional Judaism has been largely indifferent to what it considers false beliefs and otiose practices by Gentiles in other religions *provided these religions do not contravene the seven Noahide laws*. These laws define the minimum for a well-ordered, decent society. They are six prohibitions, respectively, on idolatry, various forms of sexual licentiousness, murder, blaspheming God, stealing, and eating part of a live animal, and a positive obligation to establish just courts of law.[13] Regarding Islam, for example, as far as Judaism is concerned, a non-Jew is permitted to believe that Muhammad is a prophet to whom an

---

10 Joel Kaminsky has given a superb account of the centrality of chosenness (which he calls "election") in the Hebrew Bible. See Joel S. Kaminsky, *Yet I Loved Jacob: Reclaiming the Biblical Concept of Election* (Nashville: Abingdon Press, 2007), chapters 1-4.

11 Hans Kung, *The Church* (Garden City: Image Books, 1976), 159.

12 A classic example of such a position is John Hick, *An Interpretation of Religion: Human Responses to the Transcendent* (New York: Macmillan, 1989).

13 For a classic treatise on the Noahide Laws, see David Novak, *The Image of the Non-Jew in Judaism: An Historical and Constructive Study of the Noahide Laws,* (Lewiston, NY: Edwin Mellen Press, 1983).

angel appeared and dictated the Koran, provided that the *Koran* and the *Hadith* do not violate the seven laws given to the children of Noah. And, it is a commonplace view in Judaism that Islam does not constitute idol worship.[14]

On the other hand, Jewish history has been ambivalent regarding Christianity. Maimonides ruled unequivocally that Christianity was idolatry. He implies that the doctrine of the Trinity is idolatrous because it involves worship of others in addition to the one God, and also implies that the incarnation is idolatrous and in any case a logical impossibility.[15] Following Maimonides' ruling, Orthodox Jews commonly will not enter a church on the grounds that it is a place of idol worship.

The clearest opposing view on Christianity was that of Rabbi Menahem ha-Meiri, who lived in the fourteenth and fifteenth centuries. Ha-Meiri roundly declared Christianity not to be idol worship since it believes in one Creator and since it fulfills his other requirements for fostering a decent human society. Increasingly, contemporary liberal traditional Jews adhere to this attitude toward Christianity.[16]

As for me, my exposure to religions other than Judaism and to sincere adherents of those religions has forced on me an attitude of respect and appreciation for various spiritual values I see there.

From the *Confessions* of Augustine, I have learned of the quest for God and of God's unexpected ways of bringing people to Him. Augustine's mother, a Christian, prays with all her heart that God not let Augustine leave North Africa for Rome, lest he befriend Manicheans there and be

---

14 An extreme expression of this attitude occurred when a well-known Orthodox Rabbi residing in Jerusalem ruled that if a Jew is in a place where there is no synagogue in which to pray, but there is a mosque nearby, that person should go to the mosque to recite the Jewish prayers.

15 I am indebted for this information to Daniel Lasker, "Tradition and Innovation in Maimonides' Attitude toward Other Religions," in Jay M. Harris, ed., *Maimonides after 800 Years: Essays on Maimonides and His Influence* (Cambridge, MA and London: Harvard University Press, 2007), 167-182.

16 For a study of ha-Meiri on Christianity, see Moshe Halbertal, "'Ones Possessed of Religion': Religious Tolerance in the Teachings of the Meiri," *The Edah Journal*, 1:1, 2001. Similarly, traditional Jewish authorities have held Buddhism to be idolatry, based on the prominent presence of Buddha statues in Buddhist practice and the worship of Buddha in some Buddhist traditions. However, while these authorities may have well understood the practices of much of Buddhism, there are forms of Buddhism that do not worship the Buddha, and these authorities certainly have failed to understand Zen, which dared say, "If you meet the Buddha on the way, kill him!" In any case, the Meiri's attitude to Christianity might be made to cover Buddhism as well. For more on Buddhism see the next chapter. See also my, "Judaism and Buddhism," in Alon Goshen-Gottstein and Eugene Korn, eds., *Judaism and World Religions* (Littman Library: Oxford University Press, 2012).

lost to Christianity. Augustine writes that God "answered her prayers" and sent him off to Rome—where he converted to Christianity and ultimately became Saint Augustine. I am profoundly moved by this story, in spite of the fact that I believe that Jesus was not divine and that there is no divine Trinity.

The great thirteenth century Islamic Sufi mystic, Rumi, told of a disciple who cried "Allah" over and over again, but heard no reply from God saying, to him, "Here I am." In a dream the disciple saw the master, who told him he was wrong to think that God had not answered him. "Nay," said the master, "God says: 'That "Allah" of thine is my "Here I am," and that supplication and grief and ardor of thine is my messenger to thee.... Beneath every "O Lord" of thine is many a "Here am I" from me.'"[17] Thus have I learned that when I call to God again and again and hear no reply, I should not think that God has not answered my call. On the contrary, God's reply to me was in my very call. This teaches me a lesson of what it means for God to be close to me, despite the fact that I do not believe that the Quran is God's word, nor that Muhammad was God's prophet.

From the *Heart Sutra* and the *Diamond Sutra*, from Dogen and the Sixth Patriarch, and from the writings of Thich Nhat Hanh, I have learned of dimensions of holiness that I would not have imagined as a Jew. Buddhism has deeply affected my spiritual inwardness even though I do not believe in the divinity of the Buddha or in the cycle of rebirth.

From the classic Tao work, *Tao Te Ching*, I have learned what it might be like to flow like a mighty river, while remaining calm and still. This, in spite of the fact that I can't tell you the difference between ying and yang.

Sri Ramakrishna, the "Hindu," has driven home to me how to see God everywhere, even in the lowly cat and in the charging elephant. That was why he fed to the cat the offering that had been given to the Divine Mother, and was why he taught that it is really God who was elephant-charging. And Ramakrishna also wisely taught me that although the elephant is God, I should run like hell out of the way of the charging animal! This I have internalized in spite of the fact that I do

---

17   As quoted in Annemarie Schimmel, *Mystical Dimensions of Islam* (Chapel Hill: University of North Carolina, 1975), 165-166.

not believe in Krishna or "The Mother."[18]

I can only judge that those Jews who have little or no appreciation of other religions suffer from one or more of the following: (1) They are ignorant of the more sublime literature in these religions, (2) They have a negative attitude toward other religions because of the part Christianity has played in the persecution of Jews, thus seeing all religions as enemies of the Jews and Judaism, and (3) They are unable to admit that great spiritual force can be embedded in what Judaism sees as a religion with at least one false core doctrine.

My criterion B comes down on the side of Meiri for Christianity, and in general calls for advancing a respectful and appreciative attitude, *in principle*, toward other world religions. This entails a basic appreciation for and encouragement of other religions, while at the same time being able to criticize other religions when warranted. One must think critically about religions other than one's own, just as one might think critically about one's *own* religion.

Criterion C

Criterion C is meant to reject superiority of the Jews or the degrading of non-Jews in two ways. First, it rejects that the Jews were chosen *because* they were (all things considered) superior to all other nations in the eyes of God, for example, genetically. And it rejects saying that the Jewish people *became* (all things considered) superior to all other nations in the eyes of God after being chosen.[19]

Perhaps not all nations are created equal in abilities and capacities. In any case, superiority strikes me as an unsatisfactory reason for God to choose the Jews even if they were superior. If anything, my God would most likely choose a nation more in need of God's love and mercy than a superior one.

As for overall superiority in the eyes of God as a result of being cho-

---

18   On Ramakrishna see: M. *The Gospel of Ramakrishna*, translated by Swami Nikhilananda (Mylapore: Sri Ramakrishna Math, 1964).

19   There are traces of my position in rabbinic literature. For example, there is this "Pauline"-type declaration: "Whether Jew or Gentile, whether man or woman, whether male slave or female slave, according to their actions does the Holy Spirit rest upon them." *Tana Divei Eliyahu Rabbah*, 10. Marc Hirshman has elaborated on a similar rabbinic position in *Torah for All Persons: A Universal Approach in Tanaitic Literature and Its Relationship to Wisdom of the Nations* (Hebrew) (Israel: Israel Ministry of Defense, 1999).

sen, it is important to me to deny this. My desire is to find an approach to chosenness that does not in any way imply supremacy to the Jews even after having been chosen, yet keeps a meaningful concept of chosenness alive.

Criterion D

In the first place, Criterion D, having God at the center, is meant to fend off super-liberal views of Judaism where God does not appear at all, or in which God hovers so far from the center of one's concerns, so close to the outer edge, that, as Kierkegaard remarked in a different context, "God becomes an invisible vanishing point, a powerless thought."[20]

When saying that God is in the center, I mean that ultimately all religious content and behavior must be perceived as relating us to God, and that there should be an active awareness of this purpose in the religious life. To say that religion must relate us to God can include any number of attitudes, including serving God, worshiping God, obeying God, being in fellowship with God, becoming aware of God's presence, of God's absence, imitating God, etc. I also mean to exclude the idea that the purpose of religion is to serve humanity. While I do not deny that religions have elements of great benefit to human beings, and that God would have included this in God's purposes, these should not occupy the center of the religious life all by themselves. The ultimacy of God is what I am concerned with, rather than the ultimacy of humankind.

I will not dictate the details of what "God" must mean. Surely, we should allow much latitude here. In the previous chapter, I gave one conception of God, and of course there are others. However, my criterion D should be taken, at the least, to disallow a naturalistic reduction of the notion of God, one that does God in and lays God to rest quietly, without blood. My God is not reducible to a mere cosmic process or to the system of the laws of nature, or the like. My God is a robust metaphysical reality. But, similar to my remark in a previous chapter, you need not accept my view of God as a metaphysical reality in order to agree with Criterion D. You may be a fictionalist about God, for ex-

---

20   Søren Kierkegaard, *Fear and Trembling* (Princeton: Princeton University Press, 1970).

ample, as long as you talk a language in which "God" figures centrally.

Criterion E

I turn to criterion E, that an acceptable view of Jewish chosenness should make use of central traditional Jewish sources. I mean to insure that a new proposal about what it means for the Jews to be chosen is seen as growing organically out of the Judaic tradition, and not as just a new story that is out of touch with an old one. To fulfill that requirement, Jewish tradition need not endorse my view (it doesn't), nor need my view even be consistent with what might be a prevalent understanding of that tradition. But it should be able to express at least some central ideas and some central values found in that tradition. Criterion E belongs to the "traditional" as well as to the "critical" part of my "critical traditionalism."

Criterion F

My last criterion, F, says that a view of chosenness should have plausibility, from a Judaic perspective, in light of what we know of the contemporary world and what we can reasonably expect for the future. We live in a world greatly changed from the world of even a century ago. In 1898, the first international Urban Planning Conference convened in New York City. It quickly disbanded because it saw no possible solution to the greatest problem facing urban centers: the horse-manure crisis. Horses were dropping so much manure in the city streets that in a few years, with the inevitable increased use of horses, cities would be buried in manure.[21] Our sense of the role and place of the Jews in today's world should not be appropriate to a world analogous to the world when beset by the problem of horse manure. It should be geared to a realistic understanding of future possibilities. In giving meaning to the idea of the Jews as God's chosen people we should be making claims for the Jews' role in the world that square with the new realities of life.

The upheavals of the twentieth century require a new look at the boundaries of tradition. There exist and have existed many variations

---

21   For details on this historical crisis, see: http://www.skytran.net/18EnergyEff/Images-Energy/
ACCESS30-HorseToHorsePower.pdf, accessed on August 14, 2011.

on traditional Judaism. It is time for yet another. My proposal is not aimed at interpreting what chosenness has meant in the past, but what it might mean in the future, given our situation in the contemporary world.

In the next chapter, I apply these criteria to an array of views on what it means for the Jews to be God's chosen people. While some of these views have much merit, in the end they are not adequate to the task of defining what Jewish chosenness might mean in the future.

III

Views of Chosenness

Now that I have presented the criteria for an acceptable view of Jewish chosenness, I turn to critique a sampling of views that exist about Jewish chosenness. By the nature of things I could not possibly canvas all of the interpretations that have been given. I have chosen to discuss those that have been most promulgated in the tradition, as well as some of more recent origin that deserve attention. Of those I consider, some of them I will have to decline to accept at all, while others I believe to be partially acceptable but not sufficient to fulfill all of my criteria. They must be supplemented by further considerations, which I offer.

View 1: *Chosenness as an Accident of History*

In an impressive scholarly study, Reuven Firestone has explored what he calls the "meaning of Chosenness in Judaism, Christianity, and Islam."[1] His starting point is that in the ancient Near East, gods were local, each in a special relationship with a tribe or a people, whom the god protected in exchange for their service to the god. Naturally, argues Firestone, such an arrangement with a god conferred upon the tribe the status of a special, "chosen people," in relation to *that* god. Just so, at the start, the "god" of the Israelites, YHWH, was a local divinity who granted protection to this small people in exchange for their homage. They were *this* god's chosen people. When later this very god, YHWH, became in the eyes of the Israelites the "God" of all the cosmos, the notion of being the chosen people was simply expanded, now grafted onto the God who ruled all peoples. This is how we ended up with the Jews being "God's" one chosen people. In their times, Christianity and Islam had to claim "chosenness" status for themselves in order to claim

---

1   Reuven Firestone, *Who Are the Real Chosen People: The Meaning of Chosenness in Judaism, Christianity, and Islam* (Woodstock, VT.: Skylight Paths Publishing, 2008).

superiority over the previous religion or religions that had staked out that claim. Firestone concludes, "Chosenness and monotheism are not the same thing, nor are they dependent on one another. Their intimate relationship is actually an accident of the history of the religions that emerged out of the ancient Near East.[2]

Firestone ends his study with the following declaration:

> Every religion is unique, and each has access to wisdom, including wisdom about God and eternity. But no religion has wisdom about which all of us can agree, and none has the right to be confident that it has a monopoly on truth.[3]

Since I am an open exclusivist, as explained earlier, I concur wholeheartedly with his sentiment that no religion can be "confident that it has a monopoly on truth." My open exclusivism is open to learning from other religions and does not claim a monopoly on truth. Firestone's mistake is to equate the doctrine of Jewish chosenness with *closed* exclusivism, with the view that there can be no truth in another religion that is not already in my religion. However, there are ways to endorse both Jewish chosenness *and* open exclusivism. I will be presenting my own way of doing this, and further on in this chapter I refer to other ways as well (which I critique for my own reasons). If Firestone is concerned to eliminate the historical abuses of the chosenness doctrine he can do so without giving up on that doctrine itself.

Firestone is not advocating open exclusivism in the above quotation. In private correspondence he has indicated to me that he intended to endorse religious pluralism. Each religion and each people is unique in its own way, and therefore, no one can be said to be God's "chosen." Therefore, Firestone's view goes against my criterion A, which takes the doctrine of the Jewish people being chosen as a core truth of exclusivist Judaism, and says that any religion that denies it has at least that one false belief. My interest is to show that one can be an exclusivist and yet hold a viable understanding of what it means for the Jews to be God's chosen people.

---

2   Firestone, 147.
3   Firestone, 150.

Firestone's pluralism seems to be motivated by two concerns. One is that chosenness is an accident of history, and therefore should not be taken seriously, and the second is that chosenness doctrines lead to strife and much human suffering. As for the first, the historical facts that Firestone marshals are consistent with a divine plan to have the complex of Near Eastern religions issue into a true belief in the chosenness of the Jewish people. God, it could be said, readied the Israelite nation for their being chosen by guiding history so that chosenness was a notion in the air from other gods and cultures. Other ways can be found to nail down the consistency. And as for the second, moral concerns, I hope to show that Firestone's concerns can be attended to in an exclusivist framework. A doctrine of the Jewish people as God's chosen people need not be interpreted so as to be even remotely a source of violence and strife by Jews or non-Jews.

View 2: God's Special Love for the Jews

The Hebrew Bible says that God chose the Israelites because of God's love for them. Deuteronomy 7:7-8 says:

> Of all the peoples on earth God chose you to be His treasured people.... Because the LORD loved you, and because He would keep the oath that He swore unto your fathers, has the LORD brought you out with a mighty hand, and redeemed you out of the house of bondage, from the hand of Pharaoh king of Egypt.

Deuteronomy 10:15 declares:

> It was to your fathers that the Lord was drawn in His love for them, so that He chose you...

And Deuteronomy 14:1-2 states:

> You are the children of the LORD your God: you shall not cut yourselves, nor make any baldness between your eyes for the dead. For you are a holy people unto the LORD your God, and the LORD has chosen you to be His

own treasure out of all peoples that are upon the face of the earth.

View 2 dominates in the ancient rabbinic literature, as standardly interpreted, taking these verses to be declaring that God loves *only* the Jewish people, or, at least, loves them *far more* than anybody else.[4] Here is a rabbinic text attesting to God's love solely of the Jews, by having God say to the Jewish people:

> You have made me the sole object of your love,[5] as it is written, "Hear Israel, the Lord Our God, The Lord is One," (Deuteronomy 6:4) And I make you the sole object of my love, as it is written, "Who is like your people Israel, one nation on earth. (I Chronicles 17:21). (Talmud Hagigah, 3a-3b)

In other Rabbinic texts we find that Gentiles have no share in the World to Come (Leviticus Rabbah 13:2), that the Ten Commandments spell "death" to the Gentiles (Leviticus Rabbah 1:11), that the Jews are akin to God's wife and the Gentiles to God's concubine (Leviticus Rabbah 1:13), that the Angel of Death rules over all nations except the Jewish nation (Exodus Rabbah 41:7), that God gave more commandments to the Jews than to the Gentiles because God loves the Jews more (Exodus Rabbah, 30:9), that God judges the Gentiles when at sleep, but judges the Jews when awake and doing good deeds so that they will get a better judgment than the Gentiles get (Midrash Rabbah, Genesis, 50:3), that all other nations are as "nothing" compared to the Jewish nation

---

4   There exists an alternative rabbinic trend more appreciative of Gentiles. Marc Hirshman has described a rabbinic tradition more open and universal in tone than those of the kind I have cited above, according to which a Gentile may study and observe the Torah and receive reward for that. Hirshman attributes a consistent position of this nature to the school of Rabbi Ishmael (second century CE), and opposes this to the school of Rabbi Akiva (first and second century CE). For example, R. Yirmiya, of the school of Rabbi Ishmael, said that a Gentile who studies (others: observes) the Torah is akin to the High Priest in stature. We also find a rabbinic text that has God telling Moses: "Do I show bias between Jew and Gentile? Between a man and a woman? Between a slave man and a slave woman? If one observes a commandment I give reward." While such passages are confined to references to individual Gentiles, and not to the Gentile nations, they do reflect a different attitude to the Gentile than do the type of passages I quoted in my first paragraph. (Hirshman, 1999).

5   In translating as "love," I follow the translation according to Marcus Jastrow. Rashi's comment would prefer "appreciation" or "praise."

(Midrash Rabbah, Leviticus 27:7), and so on.[6] Hence, God gave the Jews the true religion (truth-exclusivism) and gave the Jews far more ways to come close to God and have an intimate relationship with God than God gave to anybody else. God chose one nation because God loved only them sufficiently to want to bring them close to God.[7]

Now, no doubt these rabbinic texts issue out of the bitter repression of the Jews during much of Talmudic times. They are not to be raised up to eternal theological verities. When one person loves another, say a woman loves a certain man, this need not reflect negatively on the other men in the world whom she does not love. After all, matters of taste, background, and those "intangibles" are at work in falling in love and staying in love; but when it is God who is the lover, the situation changes quite drastically. God does not "fall in love" and is not subject to idiosyncratic tastes or preferences. God is supposed to act from perfect goodness, perfect knowledge, and perfect ability. And God, in God's infinity, has the capacity to love each and every nation and each and every individual fully, warmly, and in justice to their individual uniqueness.[8] So, while God's special love of the Jews might not *absolutely* imply Jewish superiority over all other nations, it strongly points in that direction and is most easily so taken. So, this view violates criterion C, not to imply superiority to the Jewish people or degrade non-Jews.

For a contemporary view of the Chosen People, we cannot agree that God loves the Jews and not the Gentiles, or that God loves the Jews more than God loves the Gentiles. Here, I defer to the late Rabbi Abraham Joshua Heschel who wrote: "What is an idol? *Any god who is mine but not yours*, any god concerned with me but not with you, *is an idol.*"[9]

---

6   For a discussion of this same attitude in the Middle Ages, see Jacob Katz, *Tradition and Crisis: Jewish Society at the End of the Middle Ages* (New York: Schoken Books, 1971).

7   Deuteronomy 14:1-2 also speaks of God's promise to the forefathers as a reason for Israelite chosenness. However, this cannot be given as an ultimate reason for Jewish chosenness because it begs the question of why God would choose to make promises to the forefathers of only one people. Noticeably, the Bible gives no reason for why God chose Abraham and his progeny. Suddenly, God appears to Abraham and tells him to go to the Land of Canaan (Genesis 12:1), with no prior hint of Abraham being deserving of such attention.

8   These last sentences are contra Michael Wyschogrod in, *The Body of Faith: Judaism as Corporeal Election* (Minneapolis: Seabury Press, 1983), 58-65. See particularly 63, where Wyschogrod writes, "There are those whom God loves especially, with whom he has fallen in love, as with Abraham."

9   Abraham Joshua Heschel, *The Insecurity of Freedom* (New York: Schoken Books, 1972), 86.

I endorse wholly the following declaration by an ultra-Orthodox, Hasidic Rabbi living in Israel, Rabbi Avraham Mordechai Gottlieb:

> Only one who has gone out of his mind is capable of believing that it is possible for there to be in God a national preference, that is that God should prefer a particular nation over another nation. For all of that is possible only with humans, who are capable of preferring a particular person over another person, or one society over another society. But with God who created all creatures, and who shines [God's light] and gives life to all of them, no preference is possible.[10]

In the coming chapter, I will be giving my understanding of the intricate relationship of love between God and the Jews and non-Jews, which does not imply a differential of love.

> When I recite the daily *Shema* Prayer, "Hear Oh Israel, the Lord Our God, The Lord is One," my emphasis is not only on, *"Our God."* My emphasis is equally on the *one* God, the God of all creation and of all humankind. The *Shema* prayer thus protests the idolatry of keeping God for my people, and looks forward to the eschatological vision of Zachariah 14:9 when "God will be one."[11]

View 3: Jews as Teachers about God

God told Abraham that he was to be a blessing to the nations (Genesis 12:2) and Isaiah said that the Israelites were to be a "light unto the nations" (Isaiah 42:6 and 49:6). "You are my witnesses, declares the Lord,

---

10   See the commentary of Rabbi Gottlieb to Yehuda Ashlag, *Matan Torah* (Hebrew) (Bnei Brak: Or Baruch Shalom, 2007), 33. Rabbi Gottlieb goes on to explain the basis of Jewish chosenness in two factors: the greatness of Abraham and the national suffering of the Israelites in Egypt at the inception of their national identity. Both of these can be relevant factors in chosenness.

11   We should be careful about condemning the rabbinic literature while not agreeing with it. What we are seeing is a reaction to the cruel treatment of Jews by Gentiles in their times and a defense against assimilation to Gentile culture. We who are witnesses to open, pluralistic societies and who are beneficiaries of the world's culture are more easily convinced of God's love for all humanity than was possible long ago.

and my servant whom I have chosen. You are my witnesses, declares the Lord, that I am God." (Isaiah 43:10-12). These verses and others like them are sometimes taken to be commanding the Jews to teach the world about the existence and glory of God.

In a prayer for rain, Jews say this:

> Answer us through the attribute of compassion, Creator
> of the universe who chooses His people Israel to make
> known His greatness and majestic glory.[12]

The idea of referring in a prayer for rain to the Jews as teachers to the world seems to be that the Jewish society must have its basic needs met in order to fulfill its task. So God should give them rain in order to have sufficient food to carry on their holy work.

This conception surfaces as well in the rabbinic literature, for example: "If you do not teach my divinity in the world, I will punish you." (Leviticus Rabbah, 6:5). And the Medieval commentator Isaac Abarbanel (1437-1508) writes this on Genesis 12:2, regarding God telling Abraham that he shall be a blessing to the nations:

> "And be a blessing." For [God] commanded him, that
> wither he goes he shall be a blessing for all nations. His
> sole purpose for going is intimated here, to teach them
> and make known to them the true belief, so that the
> world will be made perfect through him. (Abarbanel:
> Genesis 12:2)

Obadiah Sforno (c. 1475-1550) writes similarly on Exodus 19:6:

> You will be a nation of priests to [make] understand and
> teach to the entire human race to all call in the name of
> God and to worship Him all together.[13]

Now of course historically the Jews were instrumental in bringing monotheism to the world and continue a well-known monotheistic reli-

---

12   Translation by Rabbi Jonathan Sacks, *The Koren Siddur* (Jerusalem: Koren Publishers, 2009), 124.
13   Thanks to Eugene Korn for leading me to this source.

gion. However, if this were the meaning of Jewish chosenness it would seem that the time for the Jewish mission might have passed. As much as the Jews might have contributed monotheism to the world in the past, at this point in history it is difficult to agree that the Jews continue the same mission. "Teaching the world about God" is a task largely exhausted by the Jews for some time now, their having been replaced by Christian missionaries and Islamic expansionism. So I must reject this interpretation of Jewish chosenness in the name of criterion F, that a view of chosenness should have plausibility, from a Judaic perspective, in light of what we know of the contemporary world and what we can reasonably expect for the future.

View 4: Maimonides' View[14]

Maimonides' conception of prophesy strongly favors the idea that a person becomes a prophet by the person's own effort at connecting with the "Active Intellect."[15] Hence, according to Maimonides, the chosenness of the Jews follows from the status of Abraham and especially Moses as prophets. According to Maimonides, Abraham and Moses developed their spiritual powers until reaching a level of human perfection required for prophecy. They then received divine revelations and passed on the fruits of this prophetic knowledge to others. The people became *chosen* because they were taught by Moses. Moses did not teach them because they were already chosen. And this people just *happened* to have been the Israelite nation. Had Moses been a Hittite, say, Moses would have given the Torah to the Hittites. In effect, Maimonides changes the biblical rationale for God's choosing the Jews. For him, it was not God choosing the Jews, but rather Moses, as it were, "choosing God." The Jews simply came in the package along with Moses. So, in essence, does

---

14 My understanding of Maimonides follows Menachem Kellner, "Chosenness, Not Chauvinism: Maimonides on the Chosen People," in Daniel H. Frank, ed., *A People Apart: Chosenness and Ritual in Jewish Philosophical Thought* (Albany: State University of New York Press, 1995), Chapter 2, and Menachem Kellner, *Maimonides on Judaism and the Jewish People* (Albany: State University of New York Press, 1991). I am simplifying Maimonides' view, while hopefully not distorting it.

15 This is a controversial statement for Maimonides scholars. Yet, this interpretation of Maimonides coheres with the corpus of Maimonides' philosophy better than any of the alternatives. For an outstanding discussion of Maimonides' view of prophecy, see Howard Kreisel, *Prophecy: The History of an Idea in Medieval Jewish Philosophy* (Dordrecht, The Netherlands: Kluwer Academic Publishers, 2001).

Maimonides explain *away* Jewish chosenness.[16]

This view does away with any racial basis for Jewish chosenness. Yet, it violates criterion F, that any view have plausibility, given a Judaic perspective, in light of what we know of the contemporary world and what we can reasonably expect for the future. Maimonides thought of religious legislation as being only for the nation of the legislator. The philosopher-king legislates for his polis or his state. But, this view of religious legislation is not compelling in our day, to say the least. Legislation, even when religious, need not be confined to one people. In addition, a religion should not be thought of as the product of the insight of a single person, like Moses, but should be seen in the perspective of an entire cultural complex. Chosenness can no longer sustain itself on the grounds that a great man legislated for his people and that is why they are the chosen people.

In addition, Maimonides' view violates my criterion E. Maimonides will go only so far as to say that Christianity, and Islam, too, prepare the way for the Messiah by making Gentiles aware of God and the Hebrew Bible, but he mixes that with a decidedly negative assessment of those religions.[17]

View 5: Racial Superiority

At the extreme opposite of Maimonides is a line of thought stemming from the *kabbalah* (other views surface there as well, but tend to be secondary to the view I am now presenting), and adopted by some Hasidic figures. According to much in the *kabbalah*, an ontological duality runs between the *sitrah d'kedushah* and the *sitrah ahra*, between the "Side of Holiness" and the "Other Side." The "Other Side" is the realm of the Satan and the demonic. This same duality divides Jewish and Gentile souls—a

---

16 Menachem Kellner points out that Maimonides rarely uses the terminology of chosenness with regard to the Jewish people.

17 In a censored passage, Maimonides writes this:

> All these activities of Jesus the Nazarite, and the Ishmaelite who came after him, are all to pave the way for the true King Messiah, and to prepare the entire world to worship God as one.... For the world will already be filled with matters about the Messiah, the Torah, and the commandments....When the King Messiah will truly arrive...all the peoples will immediately realize that they had been taught lies by their forefathers, and that their ancestors and prophets had misled them. (Mishneh Torah, Laws of Kings 11:4, my translation).

Jewish soul is holy and pure, a Gentile soul is unholy and impure. Thus, the *Book of the Zohar* can deny the Image of God of non-Jews, saying that the non-Jew has the "Image of the Other Side" instead (*Zohar*, 3:104b). The Jewish soul can become corrupt but always begins pure. The Gentile soul starts out corrupt and remains corrupt to the very end. Thus, only a Jew could have an authentic connection to God and to God's Holy Torah. So, God has imparted the fullness of God's revelation to only one nation because only one nation was holy enough for it.

Moshe Halamish quotes from the mystical work *Shefa Tal* (by Shabbetai Sheftel Horowitz, 1561-1619) that, "The Jewish nation is a part of the Godly above.... The nations are from the external powers, the powers of the shells."[18] Thus, non-Jews are ontologized into a separate, demonic reality from that of the Jews. The *Zohar* can thus deny the Image of God of non-Jews, saying that the non-Jew is blessed with the "Image of the Other Side" instead (*Zohar*, 3:104b). Indeed, "The Holy One Blessed be He" cannot tolerate the non-Jews (*Zohar*, 3:42b), where the "Holy One" is a name of the centrally located *sefirah* of Tif'eret in the divine emanations. The *shechinah*, the Indwelling Presence, does not rest on the non-Jews (*Tikunei Zohar*, 69), and the non-Jews come from the "root of evil" (*Zohar*, 3:14a). On the other hand, the theme of mystical unity and harmony, which we saw earlier, applies to the People of Israel alone. They alone are "One body, one organism." (Haim Vital, *Pri Etz Haim*, Section 12, Section on Repentant Prayer, Chapter 8.) The "nations of the world" float free from this mystical organic insight.

Accordingly, we find in kabbalistic writings problems with the recognized legal possibility of conversion of non-Jews to Judaism. A non-Jew becoming a Jew should be a *metaphysical impossibility*. Indeed, as Isaiah Tishby has noted, the very notion of conversion subverts the task of battling the forces of evil.[19] When kabbalists believe conversion is possible, they usually wish to deny equal spiritual status to the convert after the conversion. Others claim that the only non-Jews who wish to convert are those who have covert ancestry among the Jews. In addition,

---

18   Moshe Halamish, "Some Aspects Concerning the Question of the Relationship of the Kabbalists to the Nations of the World," (Hebrew) in Asa Kasher and Moshe Halamish, eds, *Israeli Philosophy* (Hebrew) (Papyrus Publishing: Ramat-Aviv, 1983), 49-71.
19   Isaiah Tishby, *The Theory of Evil in Lurianic Kabbalah* (Hebrew), (Jerusalem: Magnes Press, 1993/4), 138.

concerning intermarriage between a Jew and non-Jew, this entails a cosmic act of strengthening the Other Side at the expense of the people of Israel.[20] Finally, the social rejection of the non-Jew reaches its most radical limits in the *Zohar*'s stricture not to approach physically close to a non-Jew, because the non-Jew is impure and imparts impurity to those who come close (*Zohar*, 1:220a).[21]

That Jews have racially superior souls might have seemed rather obvious to a great many Jews in Medieval Europe. Economic and social abuses, pogroms, murderous Crusades, and rabid religious persecution, all at the hands of Gentiles, made that conclusion seem palpable. This might account for the popularity of this view in olden days, although the roots of this way of looking at things are older than Medieval Europe. Alas, the racial superiority of the Jewish soul is an idea that does not pass criterion D.

Judah Halevi and Rabbi Abraham Isaac Kook, respectively, used the notion of Jewish racial distinctiveness as indicative of a Jewish obligation or mission to the world. Judah Halevi thought of the Jews as a separate ontological category above the inanimate, vegetative, animal, and human. At the same time he thought of the Jews as serving the world in a most valuable way, just as the heart serves the entire body, in virtue of the Jews uniquely possessing a special spiritual sense. Rabbi Kook can write this about the Jews and Gentiles:

> The difference between the soul (*neshamah*) of the Israelite, its essence, its inner yearnings, its aspirations, its characteristic and status, and the soul (*neshamah*) of all the Gentiles, at all levels, is bigger and deeper than the difference between the soul (*nefesh*) of a person and the soul (*nefesh*) of an animal. For between the latter there exists only a quantitative difference, but between the former there is an essential qualitative difference.[22]

---

20 For a discussion of conversion in the *Zohar*, see Jochanan H. A. Wijnhoven, "The *Zohar* and the Proselyte," in Michael A. Fishbane and Paul R. Flohr, eds., *Texts and Responses: Studies Presented to Nahum N. Glatzer on the Occasion of his Seventieth Birthday* (Leidin: E. J. Brill, 1975), 120-140.

21 For more on this topic see Jerome Gellman, "Jewish Mysticism and Morality: Kabbalah and its Ontological Dualities," *Archiv fur Religiongeschichte*, 2008.

22 Rabbi Abraham Isaac Kook, *Orot Haemunah*, (Jerusalem: Mosad Harav Kook, 1995), 156. My translation from the Hebrew. For an analysis of this paragraph and of R. Kook's view of Gentiles, see: Dov Schwartz, *Challenge and Crisis in Rabbi Kook's Circle* (Hebrew) (Tel-Aviv: Am Oved, 2001),

Yet, R. Kook thought of the Jews as so constituted as to be the divine instrument for bringing universal redemption for all people, Jew and Gentile. Each of the views of Judah Halevi and Rabbi Kook illustrates how a view of Jewish racial distinctiveness can be put to positive use and not be a source of immoral behavior and strife. Raphael Jospe calls such views "racial" without being "racist."[23] I propose to incorporate the idea of the Jews playing a role for the benefit of humankind without adopting an ontological polarity between Jews and Gentiles, as do Judah Halevi and Rabbi Kook.

View 6: Tikkun Olam—*Repairing the World*

This view enjoys popularity in some Jewish circles today, especially in the United States. Borrowing from Isaiah's references to the Israelites as a light unto the nations (Isaiah 42:6), the idea is that God wanted a people that would lead the way and be an example to the world in the task of *tikkun olam*, that is, of repairing our broken world. The idea is that God wanted a people who would excel in shaping decent societies and thus serve as a source of inspiration to others. The Jews happen to be the people God picked. The claim is not, mind you, that Jews actually live up to this task, but that this is what their role in the world is supposed to be.

The concept of fixing the broken world is a noble one, and all Jews should be encouraged to participate in any way they can to *tikkun olam*. In recent years a number of scholars, most notably Rabbi Elliot Dorff, have marshaled the case for social action in traditional Judaism.[24] However, I have three problems with making *tikkun olam* the heart of Jewish chosenness.

First, while this view often cites Isaiah's "light to the nations" mo-

---

Chapter

23 See Raphael Jospe, "Teaching Juda Ha-Levi: Defining and Shattering Myths in Jewish Philosophy," in Raphael Jospe, ed., *Paradigms in Jewish Philosophy* (Danvers, MA: Associated University Presses, 1997), 112-128.

24 Elliot N. Dorff, *To Do the Right and the Good: A Jewish Approach to Modern Social Ethics* (Philadelphia: Jewish Publication Society, 2002), and Elliot N. Dorff, *The Way into Tikkun Olam: Repairing the World* (Woodstock, VT: Jewish Lights, 2005). See also: David Shatz, Chaim I. Waxman, Nathan J. Diament, eds., *Tikkun Olam: Social Responsibility in Jewish Thought and Law* (Northvale, NJ and London: Jason Aronson, 1997).

tif for support, the theme of Jewish world mending, *as understood by this view*, is a very minor theme in Jewish tradition. The terminology of "tikkun" or fixing of the world does occur prominently in the kabbalah, especially in the thought of Rabbi Isaac Luria. However, there the term refers to meditative theurgic practices and carefully performed rituals designed to mend the rupture within the Godhead. This is about as far from social activism as one can get.[25] Where world mending is mentioned as an historical process, it generally refers to *God's* bringing about a spiritual mending in Messianic times, not to the Jews having a special mission among the nations for effecting a fixing of the world. So, for example, the daily *aleinu* prayer expresses the hope that *God* will bring about a mending of the world in God's Kingdom, not the Jews. Hence, this view only thinly fulfills my criterion B, making use of traditional Jewish sources.

Secondly, this view comes perilously close to reducing Judaism to an ethical-ecological enterprise, almost as though God simply wanted one people to lead the way in building hospitals, helping the homeless, feeding the starving, and saving the whales. In coming close to this reduction, this view comes close to contravening my criterion D in not having our relationship with God at its center. Judaism is about God; about self-transformation before God, walking with God, imitating God, and seeking to love and fear God. While Judaism certainly includes ethical behavior and social responsibility in a crucial way in our relations with God, Judaism cannot be reduced to *tikkun olam*.

Finally, and most crucially, while Judaism has had a central historical role in shaping the ethical culture of the West, in particular, in the past, Judaism *as a religious practice* has not contributed much to world-mending, in the present sense. This is especially true of the *positive* advances in modernity. And in the present, the dominant ethos of world-mending leading us into the future—such as technological advancement, women's rights, racial equality, ecology, and the like—is scarcely being led conspicuously by Jews, let alone by Jews acting in accordance with traditional Judaism. I see no reason to expect Jews

---

25   For more on Lurianic tikkun and its transformation into social activism, see Lawrence Fine, "Tikkun: A Lurianic Motif in Contemporary Jewish Thought," in *Ancient Israel to Modern Judaism IV*, edited by Jacob Neusner, Ernest S. Frerichs, and Nahum M. Sarna (Atlanta: Scholars Press,1989), 35-53.

to play that role in world history, and I find it difficult to imagine the practice of traditional Judaism to be the vehicle to mend the world, as this view interprets that term. So this view violates my criterion F.

View 7: The Jews as the Loyal "Other"

R. Jonathan Sacks, Chief Rabbi of the British Commonwealth, has written much in the spirit of this book concerning Judaism and other religions. He has also presented his own ideas on Jewish chosenness. His approach is worth quoting at length. Taking as his proof text, "Behold it is a people that dwells alone, not reckoned among the nations (Numbers 23:9), the Rabbi writes:[26]

> Why, if God is the God of the universe, accessible to every human being, should He choose *one nation* to bear witness to His presence in the human arena? This is a profound question. There is no short answer. But at least part of the answer, I believe, is this. God is wholly Other. Therefore He chose a people who would be humanity's 'other'. That is what Jews were—outsiders, different, distinctive, a people who swam against the tide and challenged the idols of the age. Judaism is the counter-voice in the conversation of mankind.
>
> During two thousand years of dispersion, Jews were the only people who, as a group, refused to assimilate to the dominant culture or convert to the dominant faith. They suffered as a result—but what they taught was not for themselves alone. They showed that a nation does not need to be powerful or large to win God's favor. They showed that a nation can lose everything else— land, power, rights, a home—and yet still not lose hope. They showed that God is not necessarily on the side of great empires or big battalions. They showed that a nation can be hated, persecuted, reviled, and yet still be loved by God. They showed that to every law of history there is an exception and what the majority believes at

---

26   Available at: http://www.chiefrabbi.org/ReadArtical1520.aaspx.

any given moment is not necessarily true. Judaism is God's question-mark against the conventional wisdom of the age.

It is neither an easy nor a comfortable fate to be "a people that dwells alone", but it is a challenging and inspirational one.[27]

Rabbi Sacks also writes, "God, the creator of humanity, having made a covenant with all humanity, then turns to one people and commands it to be different...."[28] The idea that the Jews are the "other" rings quite true when we look at Jewish history of the last two thousand years. And Rabbi Sacks is right to point out the impressiveness of Jewish sustaining power over a long stretch of history. The continued existence of the Jewish people, with the ethos of the Jewish religion, is truly remarkable.

Nonetheless, Rabbi Sacks makes too much of Jewish loyalty to God and his Torah, when he says that, "During two thousand years of dispersion, Jews were the only people who, as a group, refused to assimilate to the dominant culture or convert to the dominant faith." The Hebrew Bible is replete with the repeated backsliding and notorious sinfulness of the Israelites. Indeed immediately after receiving the Ten Commandments they worshiped the Golden Calf. At the time of the Judges, idolatry was widespread. And, at a later age, the prophet Jeremiah reports God saying, "And where are your gods that you have made for yourself? Let them come forward and if they can save you in the time of your woes, for according to the number of your cities are your gods, Israel." (Jeremiah 2:28). In fact, if David Freedman is right, the entire structure of the Hebrew Bible, through the Early Prophets, reflects the serial transgression of nine of the Ten Commandments by the people until God finally exiles them from the land.[29] In that case, the underlying message is *disloyalty*, rather than loyalty. The revelation at Sinai was a colossal flop.

A sense of disloyalty to God also pervades the Jewish prayer book, as in the declaration that, "Because of our sins and the sins of our ancestors, Jerusalem, and your people, have become a shame for all those

---

27   I am thankful to Gene Bodzin for bringing this text to my attention.

28   Jonathan Sacks, *The Dignity of Difference: How to Avoid the Clash of Civilizations* (London: Continuum Books, 2002), 53.

29   David Noel Freedman, *The Nine Commandments* (New York: Doubleday, 2000).

who surround us;" or in the lament that, "Because of our sins we have been exiled from our land." And surely in modern times, the idea of Jewish loyalty to God and the Torah is quite exaggerated. The great majority of contemporary Jews is bereft of religion or has only a tenuous connection to the Jewish religion. It is only a minority that even professes to be "religious." Today, massive unbelief and a scarcity of religious practice characterize the Jewish people far more than loyalty to God and his Torah. Neither do all segments of ostensibly religious Jewry fulfill Rabbi Sacks' vision of loyalty to God. What we have are often but thin threads of loyalty that overlap in history, giving an impression of religious continuity, imbedded in a widespread distance from the religion.

While Jewish identity maintains strength in Israel, the United States, and elsewhere we should not confuse ethnic identity with loyalty to God and the Torah. Looking ahead, and not back, it is not easy to see the Jewish nation, *as a nation*, acting as Rabbi Sacks represents them as a *nation* loyal to God and the Torah. Our concept of Jewish chosenness must not depend upon a miraculous and sudden change of heart on the part of the great majority of Jews who will promptly begin to observe the Sabbath and dedicate themselves to making a decent Jewish society. So this view runs afoul of my criterion F, that a view of chosenness should have plausibility, from a Judaic perspective, in light of what we know of the contemporary world and what we can reasonably expect for the future.

My own proposal on Jewish chosenness in the next chapter will focus on God's act of choosing the Jews, and not upon the Jews' response to having been chosen. But I am getting ahead of my story.

A second problem with this proposal is that aiming the spotlight on "otherness" and "a people apart" carries the danger of isolation from other peoples, together with a sense of superiority toward them. Today what we need is a way of preserving Jewish "otherness" while vigorously promoting openness to others and finding good in other religions. To his great credit, Rabbi Sacks himself seeks to accomplish this openness. Yet, the danger of xenophobia lurks in the background of a stress on Jewish otherness and is threatening to a fitting response to our contemporary world, which, as Evan Fales has said, is, no longer a global village, but a global apartment house. I can do no better than to quote Søren Kierkegaard, who wrote,

> Everyone who is in despair has clung to one or another
> of the dissimilarities of earthly life so that he centers his
> life in it, not in God, also demands that everyone who
> belongs to the same dissimilarity must hold together
> with him. . . . The one in despair calls it treason to want
> to have fellowship with others, with all people.[30]

So this proposal threatens to make trouble for my criteria D and E.
(Of course this is the opposite of Rabbi Sacks' intention.) I need something more than Jewish "otherness" to insure a greater chance of compliance with my criteria.

View 8: Opening of the Covenant

Michael Kogan has advanced a new version of the world-mending theology of chosenness in a Jewish theology of Christianity.[31] Kogan writes,
"The mission of Israel is world redemption" (205, 227), which he strongly
equates with "universal morality," "often referred to as the Kingdom of
God" (205). This morality gets translated for Kogan into "the dignity
of every human being, the sanctity of all life, justice for all persons and
peoples, and reverence for the earth, our home" (11). In other words, it
was for civil rights, national self-determination, and ecology that the
Jews were chosen for a covenant with God. I have already given reasons
why I do not accept such a view of the Jews' mission in contemporary
times. This tends to reduce Judaism to social action and lacks in realism.
What remains of interest, though, is Kogan's view of Christianity as a
way of relating to other religions with respect.

Kogan believes that God opened the Jewish covenant to the Gentiles
through Jesus and Paul: "The God of Israel has acted through the
Christian founder to open the covenant via a new revelation to the
world" (13, 34). For him, then, Christianity is one form of "Jewish
outreach" and Jesus' life an "aspect of Israel's redemptive work" (68,
131, 149, 171). To Kogan, Jews have no reason to deny the truths of

---

30 Søren Kierkegaard, *Works of Love*, edited and translated with Introduction by Howard V. Hong and
Edna H. Hong (Princeton: Princeton University Press, 1995), "You Shall Love the Neighbor," 73.

31 Michael S. Kogan, *Opening the Covenant: A Jewish Theology of Christianity* (New York: Oxford
University Press, 2008).

Christianity, including incarnation and resurrection, since Christianity is solely for the Gentiles. Jews should even engage in mutual influence with Christianity for the betterment of the two religions.

As a description of the past, of course, there are insurmountable difficulties for Kogan's theology of Christianity as an opening of the Covenant to the Gentiles. Jews had no idea that this was the purpose of Christianity. Generally, Jews thought of Christianity as demonic, and almost all Jews believed Christianity to be pagan idol worship. Furthermore, all that time Christians had not the vaguest idea that Christianity was God's way of opening the Jewish covenant to them. They were convinced that Satan had blinded the Synagogue to the obvious fact that the Church had come to supersede Judaism with a New Israel and a New Covenant. For most of their history, Christians believed the Jews were an accursed people allowed to exist only as a living reminder of the wretchedness of those who would deny Christ.

That critique will not stand, however. We need not take Kogan to be making a claim about the *past* understanding of the relationship between Judaism and Christianity. We can understand him as proposing a reform in that understanding for the future. From now on, he would be saying, the Jews should see Christianity as a new divine revelation, which took the form of incarnation, crucifixion, and resurrection, for the purpose of opening the covenant to the Gentiles.

Unfortunately, I find a number of problems with Kogan's proposal. The first is that if Christianity was an opening of the covenant to the Gentiles, while the Jewish covenant was to remain in place, it is hard to understand why God did not open God's covenant to the Gentiles by way of a Gentile, or at least by a clearly pious Jew. Instead, the opening was by two Jews, Jesus and Paul, about whom there is great controversy, to say the least, concerning their personal loyalty to traditional Judaism. How could God open the Jewish covenant to the Gentiles by means of sinning Jews or Jews whose loyalty is suspect?

Secondly, if Christianity was an opening of the covenant to the Gentiles I find it difficult to give any meaning to the rise of Islam. Was it another opening of the covenant to the Gentiles? Why was another opening required? Are all other religions further openings? Even religions that predated Judaism? If I am to accept the incarnation and resurrection of Jesus, am I, a Jew, also to accept the Islamic story of a revelation to Muhammad? But, then why should I not accept the Mormon story of a revelation to Joseph Smith Jr. and the Bahai story of a revelation to Bahaullah? Am I, a Jew, to accept the Buddha's divinity? I find no good reason to distinguish here between Christianity and other religions or to accept the promiscuous implications of Kogan's approach. Respect for other religions turns into a festival of gullibility.

While Kogan's theology has good intention, it is overzealous. In order for me as a Jew to have a positive attitude toward Christianity, I do not need to think that Christianity originated in a revelation or that all its core dogmas are true. It is enough that I discern truth in Christianity, and spiritual and moral value there. I suspect that part of the attraction of a view like Kogan's might be in a super-liberal stance that says that nobody has the right to say that her religion is truer than any other. I have already given my reasons for rejecting this sort of epistemology and so I do not see this stance as a good reason to agree with Kogan, as much as I admire his attempt to advance in a positive way.

Rabbi Jonathan Sacks advances a variation on Kogan's idea when he writes that, "The idea that one God entails one faith, one truth, one covenant, is countered by the story of Babel."[32] I understand Rabbi Sacks to be advocating a multiplicity of separate covenants with each of the world religions rather than with an opening of the one covenant to Gentiles. Some of my critique of Kogan transfers to Rabbi Sacks's position. Most particularly, I don't endorse the epistemology that seems to be driving the position: that is Rabbi Sacks's declaration that in this modern age it is impossible to believe that there is one religious truth.[33] This is worthy of endorsement if meant to deny only that there is no truth in other religions. But when it leads to the conclusion that all religions of the world are equally covenants with God, then I see little reason to accept it. Reverence and respect for other religions, I have been arguing, does not require such a far-reaching concession from Judaism. My reticence to accept the multiple covenant view will become clearer in the following chapter when I present my own view of chosenness and its implications for a Judaic attitude to other world religions.

My conclusion is that the some of the conceptions I have surveyed

---

32   Jonathan Sacks, *The Dignity of Difference: How to Avoid the Clash of Civilizations* (London: Continuum Books, 2002), 200. I am indebted to Marc Shapiro for leading me to this quote. Rabbi Sacks modified his position in a second edition, due apparently to pressure from conservative religious groups. See, Marc Shapiro, "Of Books and Bans," *The Edah Journal*, 3, 2 (1992/93).

33   See Sacks, 10.

of the Jews as the chosen people have something to contribute to a viable concept for our days. Yet, none make it through all of the criteria I have set up for acceptability. In the following chapter—with "fear and love"—I turn to my own proposal of what it might mean for the Jews to be God's chosen people.

IV

For God's Kindness Has Overwhelmed Us: Jews and the Nations of the World

I

In his *Philosophical Fragments*, Søren Kierkegaard presented a most poignant parable about a king who falls in love with a humble maiden. The king fears he will overwhelm the maiden with "all the pomp of his power," thereby depriving her of her autonomy and sense of self-worth so necessary for their mutual love. So the king limits himself, and himself becomes a humble servant, so as to join with her in love freely given. Just so, says Kierkegaard, "God picks His steps . . . lest he trample human beings in the dust." And just so, God limits Himself so that people will come to him freely. For Kierkegaard this thought leads into a kenotic theology of the incarnation, where God becomes a humble man so as to enter into relationship with other human beings in "freedom and joy." God becomes the man Jesus who walks and talks among humanity as one of them, fostering a love that God could not get in any other way. This is not a pose or a trick, for God, for Kierkegaard, really does become a man, becomes a humble servant to be, as it were, with the maiden.

The principle of Kierkegaard's parable is that God will not force God's self onto a person by depriving her of her freedom with regard to choosing God. A number of Christian philosophers agree with the spirit of Kierkegaard's parable. They argue that God must be "elusive" and not overwhelm so as not to rob people of their morally significant response to the Divine. Thus, Ronald Hepburn wrote that,

> If God were incontrovertibly revealed, then our belief would be constrained, our allegiance forced, and no place would be left for free and responsible decision whether to walk in God's ways and to entrust oneself to him in faith. Divine elusiveness is a necessary condition of our

being able to enter upon properly personal relations with God.[1]

And Michael Murray wrote,

> To preserve the exercise of robust, morally significant free will, God cannot provide grand-scale, firework displays in an effort to make His existence known.[2]

C. Stephen Evans has expressed an idea in this spirit in a principle he calls the "Easy Resistibility Principle."[3] According to this, God makes it easy for people to resist Him. Says Evans,

> Those who do not wish to love and serve God find it relatively easy to reject the idea that there is knowledge of God. The plausibility of this principle stems from the assumption that God wants the relation humans are to enjoy with him to be one in which they love and serve him freely and joyfully.[4]

In this way, Evans explains why God does not provide strongly indicative natural signs of God's presence in the world. God abides by the principle of Easy Resistibility. Yet, says Evans, God does make His presence accessible to those who wish to know him. Evans makes of this the "Principle of Wide Accessibility," according to which God makes it *possible* at least for humans to come to know his existence. Still, the signs have to be read and a person must enter freely into a relationship with God.

Also, the Christian theologian, Paul K. Moser, in a book entitled, *The Elusive God*, has argued extensively that God would grant a non-coercive offer of fellowship to humans in which we are free to respond to God in

---

1   Ronald W. Hepburn, "From World to God," *Mind*, 72: 40-50.

2   Michael Murray, "Coercion and the Hiddenness of God," *American Philosophical Quarterly* 30: 37.

3   C. Stephen Evans, *Natural Signs and Knowledge of God: A New Look at Theistic Arguments* (New York: Oxford University Press, 2010).

4   This idea seems to surface in the Quran, where God says to Muhammad, "Had your Lord willed, all the people on earth would have believed. Do you want to force the people to become believers?" 10:99/100. As I note below, though, this topic is quite complex in Islam.

love.[5] God thus approaches us with a "call," unlike "the coercive evidence of a splitting headache that just won't go away." God's call

> ...may intrude a bit into our experience, say in conscience, but it can readily be overlooked, ignored, suppressed, or dismissed by us, because it's intended by God not to coerce a will . . . but to be willingly received by humans. In particular, it's designed to woo or invite us rather than to force or dominate us.[6]

These Christian philosophers, as well as others, testify to the fundamental way God relates to the world.[7] The same idea surfaces in Jewish thought at times. The *Sefer Hachinuch* gives the following explanation for the Biblical commandment to keep a fire burning on the altar in the Tabernacle. (Mitzvah 132):

> We and every wise person knows that in great miracles which God performs with His goodness to people, He will all ways do them in a way of hiddenness, so that it appears somewhat as though they are plainly natural, or nearly natural. Even with the miracle of the parting of the Red Sea, which was a demonstrative miracle, it is written that God moved the sea by way of an easterly wind the entire night, making the sea dry. For that reason, we are commanded to burn a fire on the altar, even though a fire would descend from heaven, in order to hide the miracle [of the fire descending from heaven], so that the fire that came from heaven would not be visible in its descent.[8]

The idea of this passage is that God does not want to overwhelm us,

---

5 Paul K. Moser, *The Elusive God: Reorienting Religious Epistemology* (Cambridge: Cambridge University Press, 2008).

6 Moser, 243. Divine Persuasion, rather than coercion, is a major tenet of Christian process theology. See Hartshorne, *Omnipotence and Other Theological Mistakes* (Albany: State University of New York Press, 1984) for the concept of God's power in process theology.

7 See also John Hick, *Faith and Knowledge* (Ithaca: Cornell University Press, 1957), especially 178-185.

8 My translation.

does not want to trample us in the dust, with His miracles. In order to give us the space for choosing Him freely, God hides his miracles just enough to give us a hint of his activity as well as the opportunity for us to respond to God freely.

I take this teaching of God's elusiveness to be included in the opening chapter of Genesis. For six days, God creates, pouring God's creative energy into the world, the world directly impacted by God's overbearing presence. On the seventh day, God rests. For God to "rest" is for God to withdraw God's overwhelming presence from the world so as to create the conditions for humanity to come to God in freedom. That God rests is the precondition for Eve to choose to eat from the forbidden tree and share the fruit with Adam. What it means, in Genesis 1, for the seventh day to be holy, is for it to hold the conditions for coming to God freely. (This is not yet the Jewish Shabbat. See below.)

I hope to convince you, however, that *the* formative Jewish experiences of God are a radical exception to this idea. And this exception informs the Jewish experience even today. The determining Jewish experiences of God are of *God overwhelming the Jewish people to accept Him and His Word*. God overwhelms the Jewish people, with an embrace than which none is stronger. No mere "wooing" or "invitation" for the Jews. Here is why:

1. A basic category of Judaism is "God commanding." In Judaism, God issues 613 commands to the Jewish nation, and these are expanded into a great many more laws by the rabbis. "Commandment" is such a central concept in Judaism that even the fear of God and the love of God are *considered commands* in Judaism! Franz Rosenzweig grappled with the paradox of God commanding love, and solved the problem by reducing the command to an imperative that could be uttered only by a lover to the loved.[9] As such, the imperative is a pure expression of love that could not be performed by a third party. In so saying, Rosenzweig is assimilating God's command to love God to what any lover could say to the loved one: Love me! However, this softening of the command ignores the larger scriptural context of God's commands as being far more than mere imperatives. They are the commands of an overpowering being.

---

9   See Franz Rosenzeweig, *Star of Redemption,* translated by Barbara E. Galli (Madison, WI: University of Wisconsin Press, 2005), 190-91. I am indebted to Heather Ohaneson for leading me to this source.

And it also ignores the fact that God's command to love God becomes the command of a third party religion that demands this love. No. God verily *demands* love of the Israelites in the strongest terms possible.

In Rabbinic literature, God's many commands to the Israelites are a sign of God's great love of them. So attests the following rabbinic source:

> Rabbi Hananya ben Akashia said: "God wished to confer merit on Israel. That's why God gave them such an abundance of Torah and commandments. (Tractate Makot, 23b).

God displays most vividly and powerfully love of and desire for the Jewish people in the great many commandments God "bestows" on them. No coy wooing here.

2. God redeems the Israelite slaves with numerous, shattering violations of nature in the form of plagues upon the Egyptians. God then spectacularly splits the sea to save the Israelites, following which the bible testifies that they "feared the Lord and put their trust in him and in Moses his servant." God burrows into the Israelite consciousness with an overpowering pyrotechnic display of God's activity on their behalf. No hemming and hawing, no wooing and winking.

3. God makes Mount Sinai shake, and fire and thunder drive the fear of the Lord into the Israelite nation (Exodus, 19-20). Then, God reveals the Ten Commandments not just to a leader who must then convince the people of their having been revealed by God. No. God *sears* the Ten Commandments into the consciousness of the Israelite people by revealing the commandments directly to the entire nation all at once in a shattering event.[10]

4. A Midrash expresses the lack of choice the Israelites have in being God's people. Rabbi Hanina has God declaring to the Israelites "Against your will shall you be my people." (Numbers Rabbah 2:16). This theme receives a stark formulation in the following Talmudic passage:

> Said Rabbi Dimi: [At Mt. Sinai] God turned the moun-

---

10 The plain meaning of the text in Exodus 20 is that the people heard all ten of the commandments, although later tradition limits the number of the Ten Commandments the Israelites themselves heard.

tain over above them like a bowl and said to them: "If
you accept the Torah, fine. But if not, there you will be
buried." (*Avodah Zarah* 2:2).[11]

This looks like raw coercion, not God letting the people come to God
"in freedom and joy." God veritably "tramples them in the dust," to use
Kierkegaard's phrase. I want to enlist a Hasidic interpretation of this
saying which transforms its harshness and pulls it in the direction of a
contemporary application. That interpretation turns it from a coercive
threat into an overwhelming act of love. I quote the Hasidic Master,
Rabbi Shneur Zalman of Liadi (1745-1812):

> God's love for us is greater than our love [for God]. The
> Rabbis said, "God turned the mountain over above them
> like a bowl." This means that because of the intensity of
> God's love for us [the Jewish people] He acts to arouse
> in us love of Him, so that we should not want to sepa-
> rate ourselves from Him. It is like a person who hugs a
> person [from behind] and turns him around face to face
> and won't let him go, because the love of the hugger is
> greater than that of the hugged, and so that the hugged
> will not forget the love of the hugger.[12]

On this interpretation, God is not threatening the Israelites. Rather,
God is concerned that the Israelites will not carry with them away from
the mountain a sufficiently lasting love for God. If that were to happen,
they would end up spiritually "dead" ("*there*," later, elsewhere, will be
your "burial" place). So God overwhelms them with God's own love to
spur them to respond to God in kind. God hugs them tightly (the "bowl"),
so that the feeling of God's love will stay with them for ever after. True
enough, later the Israelites then rebelled over and over again. But God
was not making it easy for them to resist. God was making resistance a
perverse response to His manifest love. As a foundational experience,
God's embrace at Sinai is to imbue all later Jewish understanding of God

---

11   Dan Baras has pointed out to me that this motif enters the Qur'an as an apparently real historical
    event. (Qur'an 2:63).

12   Rabbi Shneur Zalman of Liadi, *Mamarei Ha-Admor Ha-Zaken*, Section 195-196. My translation. I
    am indebted to Yehuda Zirkind for leading me to this text.

and the Jews with a strong sense of God's overwhelming love.[13]

God is depicted as forming a covenantal agreement with the Israelite nation, in which both sides supposedly enter freely into the contract. But the truth is that God pressed the Israelites into accepting the covenant. God did not make it easy to resist the covenant offer.

There is a popular, contrary tradition to the one about the mountain being held over the Israelites' head, that praises the people for their freely choosing God and God's Torah. Based on the declaration, "All that God says we will do and we will listen" (Exodus 24:6), the idea is that the people freely committed themselves in advance to "do" whatever they would afterward hear from God. In doing so, they acted as the angels, who are ready to perform whatever God will ask of them.[14] This tradition includes the idea that God first offered the Torah to all other nations, who rejected the offer, before the Israelites freely agreed to accept it.[15]

This latter tradition has become a rather canonical understanding of the Israelite experience at Sinai, and it might seem rather disingenuous for me to dismiss this Jewish self-understanding. However, several competing traditional sources deflect Exodus 24:6 away from that interpretation, turning the Israelite declaration, "We will do and we will listen," into a negative response to God's being about to give them a revelation. Thus is that verse left with an ambiguous legacy in Jewish tradition. Rabbi Meir states in a Midrash that when the people said, "We will do and we will listen," they had idol worship in mind. (*Shmot Rabbah 42:8*)[16] And another Midrash applies to the Israelites' declaration, "We will do and we will listen," a verse in Proverbs 24: "for their hearts devise violence, and their lips talk of trouble." The Israelites were not being honest in their declaration of accepting the Torah freely (Leviticus Rabbah 6:1, my translation).

My concept of the Jews as the chosen people adopts the view that the Israelites were showered with God's love at the mountain in order to arouse their love for God in turn. So, it favors this negative understanding of the Israelites *before* God showered them with love.

---

13 See below how to square God's love of the Jews with the reality of Jewish history.
14 Babylonian Talmud, Shabbat 88a.
15 Pesikta Zutra, V'Zot Habrachah.
16 Menachem Fisch has suggested to me that Rabbi Meir reads the Hebrew of the verse as "We will make, and we will listen," meaning: "We will listen to what we make, i.e., the Golden Calf." The Hebrew term involved, "naaseh," can mean either "We will do" or "We will make."

As I noted in an earlier chapter, if you doubt the historical truth of the biblical events I have referred to here, I would ask you to agree only that the telling of these biblical stories reflected the way the Jews perceived their relationship with God. And that was that God took hold of them and wouldn't let them go. These stories have been told and retold throughout the ages, shaping the Jewish consciousness of God.

5. The sense of being overwhelmed by God is reinforced further by the fact that, mostly, Jews are *born* Jewish. No baptism, acceptance, or initiation by parents or oneself is required. In the eyes of Jewish law, you are Jewish whether you like it or not. And there is no way out. If you are born Jewish, you can become a Jesuit priest or a Buddhist nun, yet Judaism will consider you a Jew until the end of your days. Of course, someone can choose to convert to Judaism, but in doing so one chooses to join a people whose central experience is of a divine bear hug. As long as the conversion was sincere, there is no way back. The convert will remain Jewish and commanded until the day she dies, no matter what![17] Thus does the fact of just *being* Jewish reinforce the experience of God's overwhelming the Jews in choosing them.

I do not mean to suggest that God does not also want the Jews to choose God in joy and freedom. On the contrary, this is God's fervent desire. The covenant's very existence attests to this desire. And according to one traditional source, the Jews freely chose God later in history, after the story of Esther.[18] They freely accepted what they had earlier received.

So it was, after a long period of God's overwhelming the Jews with His presence, God pulls back and wants the Jews to react in freedom in accepting Him. The opening verses of the book of Psalms attest to this ideal of choosing God in joy and freedom:

---

17 There are minority opinions against this.
18 Other sources repeat the motif of re-acceptance of the covenant. "Said Rava: 'Nonetheless, [even though they had accepted the Torah under duration] they accepted it once again in the time of Ahasuerus.'" (Talmud, Shabbat, 88a). In Joshua 24, Joshua has the people accept God's word anew. Since this Talmudic source sees a free acceptance coming only much later, we must see it as deeming the Joshua episode as less than freely given. Bruce Rosenstock has suggested to me that the return of the exiles in the time of Ezra and their acceptance of the law marks a new freely given acceptance of God and His law. See Nehemiah 10:1. See also, David Weiss Halivni, *Breaking the Tablets: Jewish Theology After the Shoah* (Lanham, MD: Rowman and Littlefield Publishers, 2007), Chapter 2.

> How blessed is the person who does not walk in the
> counsel of the wicked, Nor stand in the path of sinners,
> nor sit in the seat of scoffers! But his delight is in the
> Torah of God, and in His Torah he meditates day and
> night.

Most contemporary Jews are not likely to feel themselves compelled by God to observe Judaism. But my point is not that all Jews feel this way, and certainly not all contemporary Jews. Rather, I mean to say that, when confronting traditional Judaism, what faces a contemporary Jew is *this* sense of the Jews' formative relationship to God, reinforced for many by the lack of choice of having been born Jewish. The foundational Jewish sense of God as overwhelming the people remains the predominant lens through which to view the history of the Jews and the Jewish experience. It is in this context that the promise of the covenantal relationship is played out.[19]

II

All of this tells of God's relationship to the Jews. When addressing the non-Jews, however, God does not overwhelm. Here God does woo, does invite, issuing a *call* to come to God in freedom, a call that can be accepted or rebuffed.

Look at this Talmudic passage:

> Rabbi Yochanan said, "Every word that God said [at Mt.
> Sinai] divided into seventy languages." (Shabbat 88b)

Now, in rabbinic literature, the "seventy languages" are of the proverbial seventy nations of the world. Hence, this statement declares that God proclaimed the Ten Commandments to all the nations of the world. On my understanding, in proclaiming these words to all nations, God exhibits his desire for all to come to God in freedom. God does not compel the non-Jews as God did the Israelites. Significantly, God's call to the other nations of the world comes concurrently with God's choosing the Israelites. The Divine choice of the Jews simultaneously reverber-

---

19 I am indebted to Rabbi Francis Nataf for pointing out to me the need for this paragraph.

ates as a *call* to all of humanity. And God's call continues even today, as a rabbinic Midrash says that daily God proclaims from Mt. Sinai, "I am the Lord your God," translated, I would add, into the seventy proverbial languages of humanity.

God does not call the Gentiles to observe 613 commandments. The 613 commandments to the Jews are a function of God's overbearing demonstration of His love for them. God veritably lavishes the Jews with love. As a Midrash puts it, God says, "Take me with my Torah!"[20] And Jewish liturgy declares, *"Great love* have you loved us," for giving the commandments to the Jews. The call to the Gentiles, rather than to follow the 613 commandments, is to come to God in freedom and in joy.

III

We have seen a radical distinction between God's approach to the chosen people, the Jews, and God's approach to the non-Jews. Here, then, is my proposal as to why God would single out one nation, whether Jews or Hittites, to robustly *induce* them to accept God, while acting with self-limitation toward the rest of humanity:

1. God wants humanity to come to Him freely, so God must restrain God's manifestation of God's love for them in order to make that possible. As a result, the human race is left with no clear indication, with no obvious expression, of God's strong love for them, of God's burning desire that they choose God. So, God is in danger of being perceived as not sufficiently loving of humanity, since it seems that God is not sufficiently anxious for humans to recognize God's love for them. God must do something to prove his love to all human beings without departing from His desire that persons come to him in freedom.

2. In God's behavior toward one chosen nation, God provides a real-life demonstration, a figure, a picture, of God's desire for intimacy with *all* humanity. In God's intensity toward that nation to accept God, God says to the world: "See my passionate desire to be God to this people. Here, in my turning to them is a concrete figuration of my desire for all of humanity. Keep this before you when you discern my presence as non-compelling. Keep this in mind when I call to you but do not compel

---

20   Midrash Tanchuma, Shmot (Jerusalem: Eshkol, 1972/3), 459. My translation.

you. Don't take that as insufficient interest on my part. Here, in this nation, is proof of my wanting all of you with me."[21]

3. Thus, every act of God's love toward the people he has chosen also speaks to all peoples. Each such act is an invitation, a call, an offer by God to all peoples to receive God's love, as demonstrated by God's relationship to the people he has chosen to demonstrate his love. In this way, God is able to provide a demonstration of God's fervent desire for humanity while allowing humanity the requisite space to choose God in freedom.

4. In this way do the chosen people serve God as witnesss to humanity that God desires the hearts of *all* peoples. And this is *my* understanding of the verses in Deuteronomy, that God chose the Israelites because God loved them. God's love of the Israelites serves as a sign of God's love for all humanity.

As I have already said, this is *not* the way Jewish chosenness has been interpreted historically. Instead, most often God's love of the Jewish people was taken by the Jews to signify God's exclusive love of the Jews, or indicative at least of God's greater love of the Jews. I am proposing a new understanding of Jewish chosenness to replace old ones and other contemporary understandings. I am proposing a new story from traditional texts. And on my view, God's choice of the Jews will not be mistaken as being due to God's special love for the Jews, because the complete story I tell will be propagated. Not only do I present God as overwhelming the Jews with His love, leaving God's motive to be guessed. I tell my story about why God does this and what God hopes to accomplish thereby. The story is a "regulative narrative," which Edward Casey describes as one following the original while allowing "diversions along the way."[22]

───────────

21   In personal correspondence, Robert McKim questioned why God would choose a *nation* for the desired role. It would have made more sense, says McKim, for God to sprinkle love throughout the nations by God's overwhelming selected individuals or groups with love. I answer that a nation is able to abide by a collective religion and create a society which reflect God's love of them. This cannot be done by individuals who are sprinkled throughout humanity. In any case, I am not so interested in arguing a priori that God had to choose only a nation, rather than some other configuration. My interest is more to suggest why God, who chose a nation in fact, would have done so.

22   Edward S. Casey, *Remembering: A Phenomenological Study*, Second Edition (Bloomington, IN: Indiana University Press, 2000), 106.

Objection: If the purpose of God's choosing the Jews was as I say it was, to serve the Gentiles with a model of God's love of all humanity, how come nobody knew about it all these years? If *that* was the purpose, it was a colossal failure! Did God "forget" to let this secret out to the world? That nobody ever heard of this until now is a good reason to deny that when God chose the Jewish people, God had in mind just this.

This objection will help me to clarify the nature of my proposal. Concepts of Judaism have changed over the ages in accordance with the ability of believers to formulate them and live in accordance with them. Divine accommodation plays an important role in the development of Judaism in history. We have now reached a point in history where a new concept of the Chosen People is in order because of a new type of understanding, both moral and scientific, which God has granted to us. My proposal aims to be commensurate with that understanding, hoping to encourage a readiness to advance to a new age of realization.

* * *

The following is the explanation, promised in the previous chapter, for why in my proposal there are not multiple covenants between God and the nations of the world, or between God and religions other than Judaism. The covenant between God and the Jews is *sui generis*. The entire idea of there being a covenant, on my present proposal, is to serve God's purpose of manifesting, through the Jews, God's love for all nations. For this reason God *imposes*, albeit lovingly, the covenant on the Jews. So, there exists no covenant save through God overwhelming the recipient of the covenant. And that is precisely what God will not do to the nations of the world, whom God wants to come to God in freedom and joy.

If you like, we could adopt an attenuated sense in which there exist "covenants" between God and nations other than the Jews or with religions other than Judaism. This would be in the sense of God being ready and open to be in an intimate relationship with every human being. There would be a *potential*, waiting, "covenant" between God and other nations, dependent on their freely coming to God. In my proposal, I would prefer leaving out the notion of multiple covenants, because doing so deflects from the unique nature and purpose of God's covenant with the Jews.

IV

The history of the romance between God and the Jews has not been idyllic. It has been a mixture of millennia of Jewish responses to God in joy and with loyalty, together with Jewish resistance to God, with the resistance coming from the very start with Israelite rebellions in the desert. God, in turn, has treated the Jews both to glory and to suffering. So much suffering, in fact, that Christians could believe that the Jews continued to survive only as a sign of the misery visited upon those who would deny Christ. So much suffering, in fact, that at times Jews themselves developed a rather ironic sense of God's love of them.[23]

In light of this, I suggest that Jewish history is a complex response to God's decision to choose the Jews both by overwhelming them and granting them an enhanced capacity to respond to God with love. On the one hand, Jewish history is a story of Jews responding in love to God in light of the initial overwhelming experiences. On the other hand, it is a story of resistance born of the struggle against God's intensity, and of being born Jewish, and thus being commanded, with no choice in the matter. It is a story of struggle for freedom. Jewish rebellion is thus the price that God pays for having overwhelmed a people into serving as a demonstration of his desire for human intimacy and of ultimate divine grace. In that sense, the Jewish people have been and continue to be a *sacrifice* for God, participating in all of the joy, and all of the tragedy, of being God's chosen people.

I want to elaborate on the sacrificial nature of Jewish chosenness and on the correlative Jewish consciousness within the sacrificial mode. The continued existence of the Jewish people, through all of its triumphs and sufferings, is a living reminder to the world of the formative experiences of the Jews. That continued existence should signify to the nations of the earth God's steadfastness in staying by those to whom God has turned.[24] This is the promise implicit in the story of the exodus from Egypt.

But more. The history of the Jewish people serves as a mirror of all of human existence. Human existence has a good share of loss and

---

23 So we get the classic Jewish quip when things go wrong, as for example, "I ran like crazy to try to make my flight, and Gawt hat geholfen (God helped)...and I missed it!"

24 This, of course, is an inversion of how the Augustinian position is ordinarily understood that God keeps the Jews in a dispersed existence to suffer for their rejection of Jesus and to be witness to what happens to those who do so. (Based on Augustine's *City of God*, 18:46.)

failure, of anguish and disappointment, of suffering and defeat. This truth about human existence is mirrored in the history of the Jewish people. Jewish history has been a long litany of persecution and suffering, restrictions and isolation. But through it all Jewish history has been punctuated by God's grace shining through the tribulations of a people. The Jewish people continues to exist, and with its religion intact. In this way, the Jewish people serve as a model for how to understand one's life and how to maintain hope in the darkest of nights.

In 1914, the Jewish writer Sholem Aleichem published a play, entitled *Shver Tsu Zayn a Yid*, or "It Is Hard to Be a Jew." This, I submit, is a mirror for "It is hard to be a human being." When one looks into the mirror of the Jewish people, what one sees is that throughout the dire vicissitudes of life God's covenant will remain.[25] The controlling image here is of the burning bush, which burns but never is consumed. This image has served Jewish commentators at least since the time of the ancient Jewish philosopher Philo, who wrote:

> For the bush was a symbol of those who suffer the flames of injustice, just as the fire symbolized those responsible for it; but that which burned did not burn up, and those who suffered injustice were not to be destroyed by their oppressors.[26]

The Jewish role as God's chosen people implies a sacrificial existence that configures, but does not atone for, the fiery side of human existence with the promise of God's redemption. Hence the Jews in their sacrificial mode are a suffering servant of God's. But the Jews are not a Christ figure of Paulinian atonement. Rather, the Jews are the Israelites who endure bitter enslavement only to be redeemed in an archetype of

---

25 This does not address the question of why God allows the vicissitudes of life such free reign in the first place. I will not take up that question here. It is the classic question about God and life and most poignantly about God and the Jewish people. In what I write here there is a partial, but very partial, attempt at a theodicy concerning Jewish suffering. That is that given the fact of human suffering, Jewish suffering together with Jewish survival against all odds testifies to the world of God's grace within the afflictions of life. This is a dimension of the sacrificial role of the Jews in God's world. I do not pretend for a moment, however, that this thought justifies the horrendous evils the Jewish people have endured in their history. Neither do I address why there is human misery in the first place. Here I must be silent.

26 Philo, Life of Moses, 1:65-67, as quoted in James L. Kugel, *How to Read the Bible: A Guide to Scripture, Then and Now* (New York: Free Press, 2007), 213.

a divine promise of redemption for all of humankind.

Jewish pain is a picture of the world's pain. Our suffering, a figure of the suffering of Gentiles. Our sinning, a mirror of the sinning of others. And our goodness, a depiction of theirs. And our past redemption from the suffering of slavery, our continued existence despite all, and the promise of our future redemption are the hope held out to all of humanity.

Of course, the sacrificial nature of Jewish existence is but one side of the Jewish experience, balanced with the joy and sublimity of being Jewish and following the Jewish religion. Yet, for a Jew the joy and freedom must come through and be the result of living the sacrificial mode of service to God. It would take us too far from the task at hand were I to enter into how this complexity works itself out in Jewish religious life. But I do mean to suggest a phenomenology of Judaic religious consciousness rooted in the sense of being commanded, and overwhelmed by being God's chosen people. A sense of sacrificiality redeemed.

In saying that God only _calls_ to the non-Jews and does not compel, I must issue a slight qualification. I am aware that sometimes non-Jewish individuals have felt that God had taken hold of them tightly and would not let them go. Teresa of Avila comes to mind as an outstanding example of this. _The Catholic Encyclopedia_ writes about her, "The more she endeavored to resist, the more powerfully did God work in her soul." I recognize this as a possibility for a non-Jew, and admit that this would violate Evans' Principle of Easy Resistance. However, this phenomenon does not reflect Divine activity for Christianity as a collective. In contrast, it is the Jews as a people who have carried this sense of God's overbearing overtures to them into an entire religion, as a permanent presence in the world.

On my view, each of God's acts of love toward the Israelites and the Jews becomes a promise to the Gentiles if they will only come to God in freedom. The Exodus from Egypt speaks of a promise of redemption for all peoples in God. The giving of the Torah to the Jews signifies the possibility for all peoples to be guided by God's light if they so choose.

As I said earlier, the opening chapter of Genesis attests to God's self-removal from God's creation enough to insure its freedom. For six days, God is overwhelmingly active in and present to the world. On the seventh day, God rests. For God to "rest" is for God to withdraw God's overpowering presence from the world so as to create the conditions for humanity to come to God in freedom. This is the nature of the "Seventh Day." Shabbat, the Jewish Sabbath, on the seventh day of the week, comes and subverts the seventh day of rest of creation. The Sabbath is a sign of the close intimacy between God and the Jews, who are bound to God in the covenant: "The Children of Israel shall keep the Sabbath for all their generations, as an everlasting covenant. For between me and the Children of Israel it is a sign forever." (Exodus 31:17) Jewish tradition has taken the Shabbat to be the time in which God is most accessible to a Jewish person, in clear contrast to what is otherwise the retreat of God from an accessible presence in the world. Thus does the *Shabbat* bear a duality for the world: a movement by God to create freedom for the Gentile to come to God in joy, the seventh day, and a movement by God to bind the Jews to God as the chosen people, the Sabbath.

Why are the Jews closest to God on the Sabbath? "For in six days God made heaven and earth and on the seventh day he stopped and rested." (Exodus 31:17) Because God withdrew His obvious presence from the world on the seventh day, the Jews must then proclaim on that day that God's love for the Jews represents God's love for all. Precisely when God withdraws is the time of greatest need to remind the world of God's call, so it is then that God's loving relationship with the Jews is most important as a demonstration of God's love for all.

The Sabbath liturgy celebrates God's gift of the Sabbath day to them: "For the Lord our God has not given it to the nations of the world...for [only] to your people Israel did you give it in love, to the descendants of Jacob, whom you have chosen." (My translation) It is *because* the nations of the world do not have Shabbat, that God gives Shabbat to the Jews. The intimacy of the Sabbath exhibits the intimacy promised to all who will come wholeheartedly to God in freedom.

This concludes my presentation of what it means for the Jews to be God's Chosen People and the implications for the Jews' relationship to non-Jews. In the next chapter, I turn to the implications of this for a Jewish theology of world religions other than Judaism.

V

For God's Kindness Has Overwhelmed Us: Judaism and World Religions

Having given my conception of Jewish chosenness I turn now to the relationship between Judaism and other world religions. Some religions other than Judaism have elements of Judaism's sense of God at their foundation, but it appears to me that no other theistic religion carries quite the sense that Judaism has of how God overwhelmed the Jews at the foundational moment of Judaism.

In Christianity, Jesus ministered to the Jews, but worked no overwhelming of his audience when he preached to them. Quite the contrary—the great majority of the Jews were utterly unconvinced, despite warnings of heaven or hell, if the New Testament is to be followed. And while the later Church infamously invoked coercion and torture to save people's souls, it is not of human coercion that I speak, but of God's overwhelming presence.

Islam has a thicket of complexity concerning compulsion and tolerance, including conflicting verses in the Quran in favor of and against compulsion (In favor: "fight until there is no infidelity." Quran, 8:39; Against: "There is no compulsion in religion, for the right way is clear from the wrong way." 2:256).[1] However, this compulsion, if it exists, is again not the compulsion of which I speak. This compulsion involves the human enforcement of Islam on non-believers, at the risk of death. It does not involve a sense of God's overbearing presence in the religion's formative experiences. For example, God is not depicted as revealing the Quran to the tribes of Arabia in a grand theophany. He is portrayed as dictating the Quran through an angel to a solitary man in a cave. Other people had to be impressed by the prophet's personality

---

1   See Yohanan Friedman, *Tolerance and Coercion in Islam: Interfaith Relations in the Muslim Tradition* (Cambridge: Cambridge University, 2003) for a discussion of this in Islam.

and message to follow the new religion. Jewish tribes, for a pointed example, refused to accept the message.

Islam believes in a newborn child becoming a Muslim "by nature," with no ceremony necessary. And Indian religions (Hinduism) know of *jatis*, the caste system, wherein a person is born into a caste and can never leave it. This feature of caste status by birth is even more severe than in Judaism, since one can choose to become a Jew but cannot join a caste. Nevertheless, none of the other features of divine embrace exist on a mass scale for Islam or Indian religions as in Judaism.

In my Judaic view, *in principle* world religions other than Judaism can be freely given answers to God's non-coercive call, emanating from Sinai and onwards—responses offered within the freedom of varying cultural contexts. These other religions are developing, along with Judaism, toward the time of the Messiah, when there will be one house of prayer for all nations (Isaiah 56:7).

This does not mean that every adherent of a religion other than Judaism will feel herself having chosen to follow that religion. We know that is not so. What I do mean to say is that the religion presents, in one degree or another, its formative experience of God a dimension of coming to God in freedom.[2]

That elements of Christianity, for example, represent a freely given response to the Divine Call, grants these elements a valuable quality lacking in the foundational experiences of Judaism. A freely given response to God can be most pleasing in God's eyes. Here I draw your attention to the following Midrash that tells how beloved to God are converts to the Jewish religion:

> Rabbi Shimon ben Lakish said: The convert [to Judaism] is more beloved to God than those who stood at Mount Sinai. Why? Because all those had they not seen the sounds and the torches and lightening and the mountains shaking and the ram horns sounding, they would not have accepted upon themselves the kingdom of heaven. But this one [the convert] saw none of these and comes and attaches himself to God and accepts on

---

2   I thank Steven Kepnes for raising this point with me.

himself the kingdom of heaven, is there anyone more beloved than that?[3]

Rabbi Shimon ben Lakish speaks of converts to Judaism. The Israelites experienced frightening events at Sinai (Exodus 20:15-16), which events compromised their freedom in accepting God's Word. This is not so for converts to Judaism, who come to God in full willingness. Converts are for this reason more beloved to God than non-converts.

Let us now expand the kernel of the idea of this Rabbi's saying to all who respond to God in freedom and joy, whether Jew or Greek, man or woman, free or slave. God desires a response by the non-Jews to God's ongoing non-overwhelming call to them, as well as a new freely given acceptance of God by the Jews. These responses are beloved to God because of their dimension of freedom. In this, the Jewish people have sacrificed for the nations of the world. The Jews have endured God's overwhelming love so as to serve as a model for the Gentiles to become God's beloved.[4]

I take God's ongoing "call from Sinai" to humanity at large in a metaphorical way. The manifestation of the metaphor occurs in the intimations of the divine scattered throughout history and throughout human reality. That includes the wonders of the natural world, great spiritual figures who have opened people to the divine, private or public experiences that people interpret in religious ways, and religions that carry that call forward. To term these intimations a "call" is to affirm the belief

---

3   *Midrash Tanhuma* (Buber), (Jerusalem: Eshkol, 1971/72), 57. My translation.

4   Subsequent to my writing these lines, Dan Baras brought to my attention a traditional source that points out a merit of the non-Jews over the Jews somewhat analogous to what I am saying here. Rabbi Israel Lifshutz (1782-1860), in his commentary on the Mishnah, *Tiferet Yisrael*, writes that the non-Jews had to develop themselves and their cultures without God's direct help, but freely of their own initiative. The Jews, on the other hand, had their culture shaped by God's intervention. In that respect, the Gentiles are more deserving of praise than the Jews. Rabbi Lifshutz uses this idea to explain a Talmudic statement that ordinarily receives a harshly racist interpretation. The Talmud (Yevamot) says that only Jews are called "adam," while non-Jews are not called "adam." Ordinarily, this is taken to mean that only Jews are "human," while non-Jews are less than human. After giving several reasons why this cannot be the correct interpretation, including noting great accomplishments of non-Jews, Rabbi Lifshutz offers his own interpretation. And that is that the Talmudic dictum should be read as referring to "Adam," the first man, and not to "adam," or generic humanity. Adam was entirely formed by God, but no person was after that. (However, what was true of Adam was also true of Eve.) Adam owed everything about him to God. Just so, the Jews are like that with regard to God having formed so much of their culture. They are "Adam-like." Not so the non-Jews, who have created themselves in an admirable endeavor. (*Tiferet Yisrael* on Avot, Chapter 3)

that God wishes to have an intimate relationship with humanity, freely given and enjoyed. To dub it a call from "Sinai," is to indicate that the call to the other peoples of the world is an echo of God's overwhelming embrace of the Jewish people. And to speak of it as coming from "Sinai" is to point to God's love of the Jews as a sign of God's desire for all nations and all people.

From my Judaic point of view, then, religions other than Judaism are free to shape the contours of their response to God, as long as they adhere to the spirit of the Seven Noahide Laws mandated by Judaism of non-Jews. The "Noahide Laws" are a code for the ways of a decent, non-idolatrous society, reflecting an orientation toward the Divine. The seven laws are prohibitions on: idol worship, murder, stealing, sexual immorality, cursing God, eating from an animal while it still lives, and an obligation to set-up just courts of law. This restriction on other religions is not religious imperialism. It belongs to the criteria for recognizing when a religion really *is* (at least largely) a response to a call from God and when it might be instead (at least partly) a sinful enterprise.

Even more, the rich variegation of world religions represents, in principle, a manifold of appropriate responses to God, given the complexity of the human psyche and the wide variances in human culture. For that very reason, Judaism should be interested not only in the compliance of other religions with the seven Noahide laws, but with learning the detailed content of those religions, as responses to God's call. This is because each religion issues from a deep place in the human psyche, where there is a fundamental commonality of all humanity. Confronting other religions can thus nurture in me and in my people an appreciation of what it is like to freely respond to God in ways appropriate to each cultural world inhabited by human beings. In this way, religions of the world reciprocate to Judaism by serving as a model of freely responding to God, and of the need for adherents of Judaism to go beyond God's choosing them to a freely given and deeply self-determined choice of God. It is precisely this two-way modeling of relationships to God, and between Judaism and another religion, that Jews should nurture in inter-religious understanding.

I would not expect Christians, for example, to enter inter-religious contacts on the basis of providing to their Jewish partners a model of a religion based on a freely chosen response to God's call. I would expect many of them to think of themselves as recipients of a direct divine revelation of the truth of Christianity. But that should not prevent *Jews* from entering such contacts with that understanding. The different sides in inter-religious contacts need not have an identical rationale for such engagement. All that is required is a respect for the other side and a willingness to learn from their religious experience. Add to that the idea that a freely chosen religion has merits that a religion grounded in God's overwhelming appearance may not have, and a positive attitude to inter-religious understanding should be the result.

I repeat what I have written above. My view requires a basic appreciation for and encouragement of other religions, while at the same time reserving the right to be able to criticize other religions when warranted. This criticism could go beyond mere concern for adherence to the Seven Noahide Laws. One must think critically about religions other than one's own, just as one might think critically about one's *own* religion. Yet, each religion deserves a basic respect as reflecting a response to God's call, if so judged in sincerity.

My view also allows me to reject core teachings of other religions without judging those religions negatively. For example, I believe that Jesus was not divine and I believe that God did not dictate the Quran to Muhammad. Yet, I can appreciate various elements in Christianity and Islam as different authentic responses to God's call, responses that take shape in conformity with specific spiritual inclinations. So I invite dialogue with adherents of other religions in order to benefit from their spiritual awareness of God and from their religious sensibilities.

So far, what I have been advancing would fit well with theistic religions other than Judaism. But what of non-theistic religions? Can they be responses to God's call if they do not even recognize God? To take a prime example, how could I construe an avowedly atheistic religion as Buddhism as hearing God's call and answering it in freedom?[5] In truth, it is difficult to see how Buddhism could be a response to God. This is especially so since Buddhism has a tradition of proofs against God's existence. One of the greatest Buddhist thinkers, the founder of Madhyamika Buddhism, Nagarjuna (first to second centuries CE), argued extensively against the coherence of the concepts of God and divine

---

5 Some forms of later Buddhism are theistic in fact if not in name. Some Buddhists believe that the earthly Buddha was an incarnation of an eternal Buddha, of a Buddha spirit who is all-powerful, all knowing, perfectly good, and omnipresent. I would call such a being "God."

creation. Nagarjuna produced a battery of arguments not unfamiliar to Western atheists. These included the problem of evil, the problem of who created God, and the problem of God creating the world in stages when God should have been able to create in one sweep.[6] Buddhist thought developed into full-blown atheism, with Vasabandhu (c.400-c.480), Dharmakirti (c.600-c.660), Santaraksita (725-788), and Kamalasila (740-795). These thinkers argued for various incoherencies in the God concept, from which it followed that there was no God. Richard Hayes, an expert on these matters, writes,

> Atheism . . . is a doctrine of fundamental importance within Buddhist religious philosophy rather than a mere accretion acquired through historical accident. As such it was a doctrine for which the Buddhist apologists during the academic period were strongly motivated to find good arguments.[7]

Indeed, on the surface the problem seems insoluble. But there is no reason to remain on the surface.[8] I move below the surface by way of the following declaration by one of the greatest rabbinical figures of the twentieth century, Rabbi Abraham Isaac Kook (1865-1935):

> There is denial that is like an affirmation of faith, and an affirmation of faith akin to denial. A person can affirm the doctrine of the Torah coming from "heaven," but with the meaning of "heaven" so strange that nothing of true faith remains. And a person can deny Torah coming from "heaven" where the denial is based on what the person has absorbed of the meaning of "heaven" from people full of ludicrous thoughts. Such a person believes

---

6   For an overview of Nagarjuna on God see, Hsueh-Li Cheng, "Nāgārjuna's Approach to the Problem of the Existence of God," *Religious Studies* 12 (1976): 207-216. For the development of Buddhist arguments against God's existence, see Richard P. Hayes, "Principled Atheism in the Buddhist Scholastic Tradition," *Journal of Indian Philosophy* 16 (1988): 5-28.

7   Richard P. Hayes, "Principled Atheism in the Buddhist Scholastic Tradition," *Journal of Indian Philosophy*, 16 (1988): 16.

8   I go into this topic in greater detail in Jerome Gellman, "Judaism and Buddhism: A Jewish Approach to a Godless Religion," in *Judaism and Other Religions*, edited by Alon Goshen-Gottstein and Eugene Korn (Littman Library: Oxford University Press, 2012).

that the Torah comes from a source higher than that! Although that person may not have reached the point of truth, nonetheless this denial is to be considered akin to an affirmation of faith. "Torah from Heaven" is but an example for all affirmations of faith, regarding the relationship between their expression in language and their inner essence, the latter being the main desiratum of faith.[9]

Rabbi Kook is saying that an affirmation of faith can take the content of that affirmation so crudely that it misses the truth as much as heresy might. On the other hand, a denial of faith might come from an inner point of great spiritual sensitivity, when what it is denying is the crude formulations it has known, and rejects those because of a justified shrinking back from the crudity. Such spiritual sensitivity is akin to true faith.

I allow the possibility that Buddhists, in their proclaimed atheism, might hear in a call from God what others do not hear. In order to respond to God's call, it is not necessary to name God with the word "God," or to identify the call *as God's*. It is sufficient to hear the call. God's infinite nature may have many voices, including the sound of emptiness and of release from the bondage of existence. If the Buddhist officially denies God's existence, that denial will be an affirmation of God if what the Buddhist affirms transcends what others know of God. This is not to say simply that a Buddhist is an "anonymous theist" since what the Buddhist knows might be very different from what avowed theists know about God. But it is to acknowledge that a person can have a relationship with God without calling God by the name "God." And it is hard to see that my God would require a certain name to be given God by those who truly know God.[10]

---

9   Rabbi Abraham Isaac Kook, *Orot Haemunah* (Jerusalem: Mosad Harav Kook), 25, my translation, with amendments for easier reading.

10   A difficulty that arises here is that several forms of Buddhism seem to involve idol worship as defined in traditional Judaism. Most Buddhists worship the Buddha as an eternal being. Statues of the Buddha adorn Buddhist temples where devotees worship the Buddha through these statues. This has all the marks of idolatry. Here I would urge to go the way the Meiri went on Christianity, as outlined in the previous chapter, and restrict idol worship to pagan rites of immorality and self-destruction. Buddhism, then, would not qualify as idol worship.

The "Nations of the World"

My message is ostensibly aimed to the "nations of the world." Is this a sensible undertaking? Even today, many peoples know very little or nothing about the Jews, and surely there are still places where they have never heard of the Jews. So how can the idea I am putting forward here be a message to "humanity"? Indeed, even if every person in the world was to receive the message, very few are likely to be influenced enough to adopt it as their understanding of the Jews. So what is the point of my promulgating this in the first place? Am I not putting forward an unrealistic vision?

Here is my two-fold answer: (1) I do not suffer from megalomania. I have no illusions that the world will adopt my understanding of Jewish chosenness. Rather, as mentioned at the start of Chapter One, one of my purposes in this book is to respond positively to the challenge of the Berlin Document to extant Jewish theology. That document, if you recall, called on Jewish theologians to respond in kind to revised, newly positive, Christian theologies of the Jews and Judaism. That immediate purpose at least begins to be met by the formulation of my theological proposal and offering it as a Jewish theology for the future. (2) As I also said at the start, my real mission, unlike Paul's, is not to the Gentiles. My mission is to the Jews. I speak to those Jews in need of a theology of chosenness by which they could live a modern Jewish religious life with integrity. I offer a regulative idea, a way for Jews to think of themselves religiously and get on in our world. A regulative idea does not require its fulfillment. It can express a yearning, a dream of a better world in accordance with which a person arranges her life. Not to convince the "goyim" of our theology, necessarily, do I write, but to acknowledge a Jewish ideal, and to invite the kind of religious dialogue I have outlined in the previous chapter. My hope is that what I write here will help advance that Jewish ideal in practice.

Conclusion

Recall that a view of chosenness and Judaism is acceptable to me only if it meets these criteria:

A.   It is compatible with Judaic religious *open exclusivism.*

B.   It advances a respectful and appreciative attitude, *in principle*, toward other world religions.

C.   It does not imply Jewish superiority or imply a degradation of non-Jews.

D.   It has our relationship with God at its center.

E.   It makes use of traditional Jewish sources.

F.   It has plausibility, granting a critically traditional Judaic perspective, in light of what we know of the contemporary world and what we can hope for in the future.

My proposal concerning Jewish chosenness fulfills all of the criteria I have listed here. First, it fulfills my criterion A: in my proposal, Judaism has core beliefs all of which are true, whereas conflicting core beliefs of other religions are false. I have not committed myself on what I take to be the true core beliefs of Judaism, except for the existence of God and God's choosing the Jews. I add to that a special revelation by God to the Jews.

Criterion B is also taken care of on my proposal. I have the greatest respect and even admiration for those elements of other religions that I am able to recognize as positive responses to God's call. I do not consider deeming other religions to have some false core beliefs to be disdaining of them.[11] That is because, within the scope of my proposal, these beliefs will be part of a religion's freely given response to God's call. That is how false beliefs creep in. The value of the response depends entirely on it sincerity and its success in relating to God. As long as enough core beliefs of a religion are true *or* are of a nature to facilitate coming to God, they deserve my respect and even my admiration.

My proposal fulfills criterion C because it does not imply superiority to the Jews. I have not proposed why it was the Jews God chose to be his example of God's love to humanity. I have suggested only why God would choose some nation or other, be it the Jews or another nation. My explanation of that includes no allusion to Jewish superiority, and in fact excludes it. That is because, in my view, the Jews are but an instrument for God to achieve God's goal, which is to make known God's

---

11   Here Maimonides' distinction between true dogmas and pious dogmas can come in handy. Pious dogmas need not be true in order to orient people in the proper direction toward God. See the distinction also in Spinoza, *Tractatus Theologico-Politicus* (Leiden and New York: E. J. Brill, 1989), 223. Just so, the core ideas of a religion do not all have to be true in order for that religion to have worth.

love to all peoples while making it possible for all nations to come to God in freedom and joy.

Here, briefly, is a thought on why God might have chosen the Jews, rather than the Hittites. The *Book of Mormon* explains why Jesus was born a Jew:

> Wherefore, as I said unto you, it must needs be expedient that Christ should come among the Jews, among those who are the more wicked part of the world; and they shall crucify him—for thus it behooveth our God, and there is no other nation on earth that would crucify their God.[12]

God wanted Jesus crucified, and God in his prescience knew that no nation was evil enough to do that dastardly deed except the Jews, so it is said. So, God had to choose the Jews. Borrowing a leaf from this ignoble sentiment, perhaps God foresaw that the Jews, if chosen, would serve well for playing out God's purposes in the choosing of *any* nation. This speculation plays no part in my proposal.

My proposal meets criterion D, having God at the center. My view of chosenness relates centrally to the Jews' relationship with God as well as to the relationship of God with all humanity. Furthermore, my proposal has God as the center in the sense that the substance of chosenness is in what God does. The status of the Jews as the chosen people is the result of God choosing them. God is in the center as well when the Jews reciprocate to God by advancing God's design in choosing them.

Jews can act to advance the purpose of God's choosing them. One way of doing so is by loving God in return. Since God chose the Jews to display God's love for all humanity, by loving God in return Jews vividly confirm the love that God has for them. The supreme way of showing their love for God would be to utilize God's Torah as a means of opening their hearts, in love for God.[13]

A second way that Jews can further God's design in the contemporary world is in the love a Jew gives to a Gentile, when appropriate, acting

---

12 2 Nephi 10:3.

13 This is the meaning I give to the daily prayer asking of God: פתח לבי בתורותך —"Open my heart through your Torah: May your Torah be a means for opening my heart."

as a Jew and in the name of Judaism. The love that a Jew, as a Jew, can give to a Gentile, ultimately is God's own love. What the Jew says to a non-Jew by love is that what I offer you is God's love, mediated through God's choice of the Jews. The Jew tells the non-Jew that God loves them as much as the Jew.

My proposal well fulfills criterion E. I make use of themes that loom large in Jewish thought. I have employed the broad sweep of the Exodus story and the story of God's revelation at Sinai. In addition, I have made use of rabbinic sources as well as Hasidic sources, and in each case the sources I have quoted represent others in the literature as well. Of course, there are plenty of traditions counter to what I am presenting, but criterion E is consistent with my proposal failing to reflect what might be a mainstream view of Jewish chosenness. After all, my enterprise rejects that restriction.

Finally, my proposal takes account of the modern world and changes that have taken place in Judaism to secure a view consistent with all of that. It does not cast the Jews as world leaders in social action, but sees them as they have seen themselves in the past—as having a unique relationship with God. So Criterion F is safely home.

In the following chapter I take up two broad topics. One is a series of problems that my view must address, and the other attending to points of reinterpretation of tradition in light of my understanding of the Jews' place in God's vast world.

VI

Chosenness: Past and Future

Judaism has known many junctures at which there occurred theological reinterpretations of fundamental teachings. As I have previously stated, in the Middle Ages, Maimonides (1135-1204), David Kimchi (1160-1235), Gersonides (1288–1344), and others tried to transform Jewish thinking about God and God's relationship to the world. God was to be thought of in a more abstract way and to be far less controlling of the world than hitherto thought. In the fourteenth century, Jewish mysticism in the form of *kabbalah* came on the scene in a big way, inserting an entire new vocabulary into Judaism. There was now not only God and the angels, but structures of spiritual worlds and spiritual potencies, *sefirot*. Kabbalists evolved new rituals to manipulate these new entities for the good of the Jewish people and redemption of the world. Later, in the eighteenth century, Hasidism effected a new upheaval in Judaism, in a transformation of values from what had proceeded. Prayer was to be the center of the religious life, not Torah study; the saintly *zaddik* could raise his followers to God through his efforts on their behalf; and at times duties of the heart were to trump duties of the body.

In all these cases, their continued adherence to Jewish law and their attempts to read their novelties back into traditional texts made it possible for these new developments to claim faithfulness to tradition. Reinterpretation was a path to acceptability. Recalcitrant texts were ignored and allowed to recede into the background. In each case, there were groups who roundly rejected the new approaches as heterodoxical. Yet, in the course of history, many of these movements have become recognized as within the traditional fold, whether or not their reinterpretations have gained mass acceptance.

In the spirit of this tradition of reinterpretation, in this chapter I turn to selected crucially central Jewish texts, both biblical and liturgical, that have been given a certain range of interpretations in the past.

I advance reinterpretations of these texts for the future, commensurate with my understanding of what it means for the Jews to be God's chosen people. Lacking authority and not pretending to legislate for the Jewish people, I offer this in the spirit of stimulating awareness and discussion of the issues I have raised with hope that what I have to say will be helpful for moving forward.

The Conquest Narratives

The Jewish tradition includes many texts inconsistent, on the face of it, with my proposal of how to understand chosenness. First and foremost are biblical stories of the Israelites' conquest and destruction of various nations in the Land of Canaan and its vicinity. In Deuteronomy 7, God commands the utter extermination of the peoples living in Canaan, and in Exodus 17 and Deuteronomy 25, God commands an eternal battle to exterminate Amalek. If God's love of the Israelites was supposed to be a sign of God's love of all peoples, then we can hardly expect God's love of the Israelites to be expressed in God's killing off a bunch of other nations on the Israelites' behalf. Instead, we should expect God's love of the Israelites to spread outward to all the nations of the world.

I offer you three solutions to this problem. You choose which one suits you, depending on your views on the historicity of the biblical accounts. The first reply assumes the basic historicity of the biblical account and avers that the period of the Bible is a formative one in the life of the world in relation to God. In that formative period, structures were being put in place for the future post-biblical world. At this point the Israelites must be established in their land at the expense of idol worshippers and evil-doers so that the mission of the Jews as God's example to the world can begin to function and flourish. But it doesn't function fully until such a time that the Israelites are ensconced in the Holy Land and their society is established. So, inevitably some nations fall victim to God's larger plan, no doubt to be more than adequately compensated in a future life.

My second reply assumes that you believe the conquest narratives are not historical. It assumes that you believe that the Israelites came to be established in Canaan by infiltrating from the East, or by an indigenous take-over by Israelites of non-Israelites within Canaan, or by a small band of Hebrews coming to Canaan from Egypt and around which coalesced a larger population.[1] In that case, I would argue that what we see in the bible is an expression of the Israelites', and afterwards the Jews', sense of God's closeness to and utter love of them.[2] In days long ago, this sense would have been expressed by telling stories of God's destruction of their enemies and God's miraculous salvation. Nowadays this would be conveyed in other ways, including my ideas about Jewish chosenness. I remind you that I am not claiming that my idea of Jewish chosenness was then in place, which is why the Israelites' sense of God's closeness find expression in the way it did. In my proposal, I incorporate the profound sense of God's love of the Israelite nation that occurs in the biblical stories, but do not take up the meaning of chosenness some others have imparted to those stories.

My proposal about the chosen people presumes to capture the traditional Jewish sense of God's overwhelming love of the Israelites. Thus, the biblical texts I refer to above, and those like them, I take to reflect the Jewish sense of God's overwhelming love of them, expressed in stories about God destroying others for their sake. I appropriate the *sense* of God's overwhelming closeness but do not take the stories about destroying other nations to have any contemporary implications.

My third alternative is more sweeping, and leaves it an open question as to how much of the Bible's narratives, in general, are historical and how much are allegorical or otherwise non-literal. At various times, traditional Jewish commentators have given non-literal interpretations to assorted narrative passages in the Torah. This includes the stories of creation, the Garden of Eden, Cain and Abel, various genealogies, the Tower of Babel, the Binding of Isaac, and more. We today are witness to an unfolding of a divine plan of undermining the historicity of more of the Bible than the boldest of traditional commentators would have suggested. I believe this undermining is designed to force us to acknowledge other modes of understanding the Biblical text. In the past, the kabbalah and Hasidism retained literal meanings while

---

1   For the various views, see Israel Finkelstein, *The Bible Unearthed: Archeology's New Vision of Ancient Israel and the Origin of its Sacred Texts* (New York: Simon and Schuster, 2002), and *Exodus: The Egyptian Evidence*, edited by Ernest S. Frerichs and Leonard H. Lesko (Winona Lake, IN: Eisenbrauns, 1997).

2   In Chapter One, I argued against reducing events and currents in the Bible entirely to political and economic conditions.

overlaying them with mystical and personal meanings, respectively. To the extent that historicity is being undermined, these meanings might change from overlays to being central to our understanding. As with the Hasidim, in our case allegory can enter, as, for example, in reading "Canaan" as the forces within us humans (including in the Jewish people) that work against God's plan for the Jews to be successful models for humankind of God's love. The "Land of Israel" would be then the result of God's victory over those forces in virtue of God's backing the Israelites through all efforts to overcome insidious spiritual inclinations (including those of the Jews themselves). A conservative theology of allegorical interpretation would have it that those who believed the conquest narratives literally were sensing—whether aware of it or not—the truth of allegorical meanings, and expressing them as best they could, in terms of an historical conquest by the Israelites of non-Israelite nations.[3]

Divine Curses of the Israelites

Leviticus 26 recounts a litany of brutal horrors that will befall the people if they stray from God's ways.[4] Here is just a taste:

> But if you do not obey Me, and do not observe all these

---

3   Recently, a Hasidic ultra-Orthodox Rabbi in Israel, Rabbi Avraham Mordechai Gottlieb, has expressed on his website a surprising, for an Orthodox rabbi, allegorical view of biblical narratives. He writes:

> I heard from my master, may the mention of the saintly one be for a blessing, who told me the following interpretation: The truth is that biblical verses do not bear their plain meaning. The reason the [Talmudic] rabbis said that "A biblical verse does not fail to have its plain meaning," was because they were afraid that if they would posit that biblical verses do not carry their plain meaning, and would say that the biblical narratives were true only with a spiritual [non-historical] interpretation, but not in a material sense, then people would come to say that if so then they do not have to fulfill the commandments in action [but only in a spiritual way]. However, the keeping of the commandments in action is very important for a person. Therefore, they set down the general rule that "A biblical verse does not fail to have its plain meaning." This so that the matter of keeping the commandments will not be broken. (http://obshalom.org, accessed September 19, 2011.)

     In this view, all biblical narratives are allegorical in nature and all commandments literal.

4   I thank Evan Fales for bringing this problem to my attention.

commandments, and if you despise My statutes, or if your soul abhors My judgments, so that you do not perform all My commandments, but break My covenant, I also will do this to you: I will even appoint terror over you, wasting disease and fever which shall consume the eyes and cause sorrow of heart. And you shall sow your seed in vain, for your enemies shall eat it. I will set My face against you, and you shall be defeated by your enemies. Those who hate you shall reign over you, and you shall flee when no one pursues you. And after all this, if you do not obey Me, then I will punish you seven times more for your sins. I will break the pride of your power; I will make your heavens like iron and your earth like bronze. And your strength shall be spent in vain; for your land shall not yield its produce, nor shall the trees of the land yield their fruit. Then, if you walk contrary to Me, and are not willing to obey Me, I will bring on you seven times more plagues, according to your sins. I will also send wild beasts among you, which shall rob you of your children, destroy your livestock, and make you few in number; and your highways shall be desolate.

And so on. Deuteronomy 28 comes back with equally harsh curses. Here is a sample:

However, if you do not obey the LORD your God and do not carefully follow all his commands and decrees I am giving you today, all these curses will come upon you and overtake you: You will be cursed in the city and cursed in the country. Your basket and your kneading trough will be cursed. The fruit of your womb will be cursed, and the crops of your land, and the calves of your herds and the lambs of your flocks. You will be cursed when you come in and cursed when you go out. The Lord will send on you curses, confusion and rebuke in everything you put your hand to, until you are destroyed and come to sudden ruin because of the evil you have done in for-

saking him. The Lord will plague you with diseases until
he has destroyed you from the land you are entering to
possess. The Lord will strike you with wasting disease,
with fever and inflammation, with scorching heat and
drought, with blight and mildew, which will plague you
until you perish. The sky over your head will be bronze,
the ground beneath you iron. The Lord will turn the rain
of your country into dust and powder; it will come down
from the skies until you are destroyed. The Lord will
cause you to be defeated before your enemies. You will
come at them from one direction but flee from them in
seven, and you will become a thing of horror to all the
kingdoms on earth. Your carcasses will be food for all the
birds of the air and the beasts of the earth, and there will
be no one to frighten them away. The Lord will afflict you
with the boils of Egypt and with tumors, festering sores
and the itch, from which you cannot be cured. The Lord
will afflict you with madness, blindness and confusion of
mind. At midday you will grope about like a blind man in
the dark. You will be unsuccessful in everything you do;
day after day you will be oppressed and robbed, with no
one to rescue you.

Such curses do not go together with God's supposed overwhelming
love for the Jewish people. Instead, these might be the words of a ty-
rant-God whom one disobeys at great cost to oneself and one's people.
Imagine these words coming from a contemporary father or mother to
their child. We would no doubt interpret them as a form of child abuse.
So how does a God filled with overwhelming love for His children get
away with such language?

My understanding of this borrows from Maimonides. Maimonides
says that God could not tear the Israelites away from their cultural
context all at once, and thus had to gradually wean them away from
their idol worship and accompanying primitive understandings. This
was because, "It is impossible to go suddenly from one extreme to the
other; it is therefore according to the nature of man impossible for
him suddenly to discontinue everything to which he has been accus-
tomed." (*Guide*, 3:32) Maimonides explains in this way the need for

animal sacrifices in the Mosaic Code. Moses could not tell the people to suddenly stop the rituals they were familiar with, so instead they were commanded to bring sacrifices to God, as a gradual step away from idol worship.

Just so, the Israelites were steeped in a culture that utilized curses and threats within the idol worshiping of its days. It would have been too stark a transition away from idolatry had God not made curses and threats to the people as a means of motivating them to the service of God. This was part of the Divine strategy to bring the people to God in love by stages. In the olden days, when times were very different, such curses might have been imagined as issuing from a place of love and taken to lead in that direction. Hence, the curses and threats were part of the Bible just as the sacrificial cult was. Gradually these curses give way to more expressions of love and closeness. Compare the Pentateuchal curses to these verses of love and compassion in Hosia, 11:

> When Israel was a child, I loved him,
> and out of Egypt I called my son.
> It was I who taught Ephraim to walk,
> taking them by the arms;
> but they did not realize it was I who healed them.
> I led them with cords of human kindness,
> with ties of love;
> I lifted the yoke from their neck
> and bent down to feed them.
> How can I give you up, Ephraim?
> How can I hand you over, Israel?
> How can I treat you like Admah?
> How can I make you like Zeboiim?
> My heart is changed within me;
> my compassion is aroused.
> I will not carry out my fierce anger,
> nor will I turn and devastate Ephraim.
> For I am God, and not man—
> the Holy One among you.
> I will not come in wrath.

Maimonides himself comes close to this position when he writes that promises and threats are a "ruse" that God uses to get people to obey the law when they are not motivated to do so (*Guide* 3:32). The implication would seem to be that when the people would mature and know God with love, the promises and threats would no longer be needed.

God's Exclusive Love of the Jews

Deuteronomy 7:7-8 says:

> Of all the peoples on earth God chose you to be His treasured people.... Because the LORD loved you, and because He would keep the oath that He swore unto your fathers, has the LORD brought you out with a mighty hand, and redeemed you out of the house of bondage, from the hand of Pharaoh king of Egypt.

Deuteronomy 10:15 declares:

> It was to your fathers that the Lord was drawn in His love for them, so that He chose you...

Deuteronomy 14:1-2 declares:

> You are the children of the LORD your God: you shall not cut yourselves, nor make any baldness between your eyes for the dead. For you are a holy people unto the LORD your God, and the LORD has chosen you to be His own treasure out of all peoples that are upon the face of the earth.

As ordinarily understood, these verses describe God's love of the Israelites as an exclusive love, leaving the rest of humankind outside of the Divine love. On my construal these verses should be read as follows: God is portraying the love God has for the Israelites in a manner that speaks of the capacity of God to love fully and loyally to the end of times. God's capacity to love includes the ability to love each and every nation, each and every person, as though they were God's only one in the entire world. And God loves each nation and person in their uniqueness and specialness. With regard to every nation but the Jews, God waits for a response in freedom.

God of the Jews

Psalms 144:15 states: "Happy is the nation of whom this is true; happy is the nation that YHVH is their God." One way of understanding this verse is as a "possessive understanding." On this understanding, the verse says that the Israelite nation is happy because God is *their* God, and nobody else's God. This, of course, clashes with my understanding of the relationship between God, the Jews, and the nations of the world. Instead, I propose interpreting the verse as the Israelite nation expressing its happiness of making God its only God, and not worshipping idols along with God. As though they were saying: "Happy is the people who serve only God and no other gods." As such, the verse is an expression of joy that the Israelites do not go the way of the Psalmists idolatrous neighbors. So understood, the verse does not express a possession of God for the Israelite's own, but acceptance of the wonderful gift God has given them.

Psalms 117 reads as follows:

> All nations praise God! All peoples extol Him! For his kindness has overwhelmed us! And the truth of the LORD endureth for ever. Hallelujah![5]

Traditional commentators have found difficulty in this verse: Because God has shown great kindness to the Israelites, why should *the nations of the world* go and praise God? A standard reply is that when the Messiah comes, the nations of the world will be impressed with God's greatness when God keeps the promise to redeem God's chosen people.[6] I suggest an alternative interpretation. The Psalmist calls to the nations of the world to praise God for having overwhelmed the Israelites in the past with his love. God thereby has provided the nations with an image of God's love while allowing them the freedom to choose to come to God in love. Precisely because God has chosen us for the sake of the nations of the world, are the

---

5   My translation, using "overwhelmed," is not quite standard, but a plausible one.
6   For example, this is the view of Rabbi David Kimchi (1160-1235) in his commentary on Psalms and of the *Midrash Shocher Tov* (written in the twelfth century) on Psalms.

nations of the world to rejoice. I take this chapter of the Psalms as a motto for my conception of the chosenness of the Jewish people.

These selections from the Hebrew Bible illustrate how I would recommend going about understanding other biblical verses as well. We should not expect all verses to yield optimally to a magic wand of interpretation, however, any more than today we can successfully reinterpret all verses rooted in ancient cosmologies. Still, the interpretational reach should extend far enough to create a center of interpretation that orients us toward a new place and a new direction.

Jewish Liturgical References to Jewish Chosenness[7]

Many prayers in the Jewish liturgy express gratitude to God for having shown great love to the Jews by making them God's chosen people. Here are a few examples from the morning prayers in the traditional Jewish prayer book:

1. "Blessed are you, Lord our God, King of the universe, who has chosen us from all the peoples and given us His Torah."

2. "We are your people, the children of your covenant.... Therefore it is our duty to thank you, and to praise, glorify, bless, sanctify, and give praise to your name."

3. "You have loved us with great love, Lord our God, and with surpassing compassion have you had compassion on us."

4. "For you are God who performs acts of salvation, and You chose us from all peoples and tongues, bringing us close to Your great name for ever and in truth....Blessed are You, Lord, who chooses His people Israel in love."

5. "Blessed is He, our God, who created us for His glory, separated us from those who go astray...."

6. "It is our duty to praise the Master of all, and ascribe greatness to the Author of creation, who has not made us like the nations of the lands, nor placed us like the families of the earth."

---

7   For an extensive discussion of changes in traditional Jewish liturgy, from a moderate point of view, see Daniel Sperber, *On Changes in Jewish Liturgy: Options and Limitations* (Jerusalem and New York: Urim Publications, 2010).

On my conception of Jewish chosenness, these prayers, and others like them, have a dual character. First and foremost they express the Jewish sense of God's manifest closeness to them through all of their tribulations. Being God's chosen people creates a unique bond on the ground between God and the Jews, a bond Jews celebrate in their prayers. The uniqueness of the bond consists in having received God's overwhelming love, and God's sustaining them as the chosen people throughout their hardships. Secondly, the act of acknowledging and celebrating God's love of them allows the Jews to be a configuration for the world of the value and importance of coming to God in freedom. For in these prayers the Jews acknowledge on their own their desire for God and their response to God in freedom. When analyzing these prayers we must keep in mind both poles of their recitation. One pole is an expression of intimacy between God and the Jewish people, a private exchange between the chosen and the chooser, and the other pole is a showcasing of this intimacy, as an intimacy that reflects that of God and others as well.

Aleinu *Prayer*

1. It is our duty to praise the Master of all, and to ascribe greatness to the Author of creation,
2. Who has not made us like the nations of the land, nor placed us like the families of the earth;
3. Who has not made our portion like theirs, nor our lot like all their multitudes.
4. For they worship vanity and emptiness, and pray to a god who cannot save.

These are the opening lines of the *aleinu* prayer that appeared originally in the service of the High Holy days and later surfaced in the daily prayer book. I have broken it down into parts for discussion. Part 1 recognizes God as the creator and master of the whole world, including all nations of the world. Part 2 implicitly justifies God's choice of the Jews, since God is master and can choose whomever God wants. Part 3 refers to the result of God's choosing the Jews. Their place in the world and in history is different from that of the other nations. Part 4 is a rejection of the religion of others as worthless enterprises.

Parts 1-3 can be accommodated on the new conception of Jewish chosenness, although we must carefully define the intent of these lines. These parts are easily read as an expression of haughtiness and superiority of the Jews over the Gentiles. Instead, they are to be read as an adoration of God for having chosen the Jews, for having shown them overt love, and having taken them to serve God's purposes in the world. These three lines are to be read with an acknowledgment of the purpose God had in choosing the Jews as a figure of God's love for the Gentiles.

Part 4 is different. As an exclusivist, I do not mind stating that religions other than Judaism do not have all true core beliefs. That statement is consistent with other religions having some true core beliefs and, as I have been arguing all along, with their being, in principle, authentic responses to God's call. To state that other religions are false and just leave it at that falls seriously short of the attitude to be encouraged today toward religions other than Judaism. And surely to say that another religion worships emptiness is a declaration soundly inconsistent with the conception I am advancing of Judaism's relationship to other religions.

The *aleinu* prayer is ancient, with some traditionalists attributing it to the prophet Joshua. Historians tend to date it to the time of the Second Temple in Jerusalem. It is impossible to know what the original form of it was and whether it contained part 4. The Church objected to part 4 on the grounds that it was a reference to Jesus and Christianity. King Frederick, of Prussia, forced Prussian Jews to omit these words from their prayers. Eventually Jews in Europe instituted self-censorship and eliminated it from many prayer books in the sixteenth century. Yet, it remains in some prayer books. Whether or not the words originally referred to Jesus and Christianity there is no doubt that in Christian countries this became the obvious intent of persons who prayed these words.

Since at one time European Jews eliminated part 4 from the prayer book and did not consider its inclusion a matter of principle, it should not be objectionable to remove these lines from rest of the traditional Jewish prayer books. Reform prayer books and Conservative prayer books regularly do without these words, as well as many ashkenazic Orthodox prayer books. When I was growing up in the United States I never knew of line 4, and it almost never appears in prayer books in the United States. In Israel, its inclusion is common. My verdict: Self-censorship is in order here.

The "Blessing" of Minim

This blessing, in the morning prayers, originated in the time of the Talmud (see: Berachot 28:b) and occurs in a great number of variations. Here is a translation of a Medieval French version:

> May all the *minim* immediately perish! And may all the enemies of Your people, the house of Israel, speedily be cut off! And may the empire of insolence speedily be uprooted and smashed and defeated; and cast down and destroy and humble all our enemies speedily in our day Blessed are You, Eternal, who breaks enemies and humbles the insolent.

"Minim" can refer to apostates and scoffers, but can refer specifically to Christians. Ruth Langer, in an extensive study of the history of this prayer, finds medieval sources that explain the prayer as aimed against the oppressive Christendom of the day (Hence: "the empire of insolence"). She also notes that a version of this prayer found in the Cairo Genizah makes explicit mention of "Christians and Heretics."[8] In time, the wording of the prayer was changed by self-censorship to apply to "slanderers" rather than *minim*. This avoided the charge of slandering Christianity. Here is a good example of self-censorship that I advocate for other prayers that would have to be reformulated to conform to the view of chosenness I am advancing here.

Between Light and Darkness

The *havdalah* (separation, distinction) service comes at the end of the Sabbath to mark the separation or distinction between the holy day of rest and the days of the week. It includes the following prayer:

---

8   Ruth Langer, *Cursing the Christians? A History of the Birkat HaMinim* (New York: Oxford University Press, 2011)

> Blessed are you, Lord our God, king of the universe, who
> distinguishes between sacred and secular, between light
> and darkness, between Israel and the nations, between
> the seventh day and the six days of work.

This formulation exists in Orthodox and Conservative prayer books. As early as 1895 it disappeared from the Reform prayer book, and remains generally absent for Reform Jews.

This prayer originates in the Talmud (Pesachim 103b), which has a longer form of the prayer, adding to the above:

> between the pure and the impure, between the sea and
> the dry land, between the lower waters and the upper
> waters, and between the priests and the Levites and
> Israelites.

Each of the distinctions in the two formulations corresponds to a verse or verses in the Torah in which God separates one thing from another. The separation between the Jews and the other peoples occurs at Leviticus 20:26:

> You shall be holy unto Me; for I the LORD am holy, and
> have set you apart from the peoples, that you should be
> Mine.

I propose two approaches to the problematic aspects of this prayer, one specific and one wholesale for all similar prayers. Here is a fresh reading of this specific prayer: While the *havdalah* prayer and the verses it bases itself on might make us believe that each of the distinctions is categorical and fixed, later Jewish literature suggests that at least some of the distinctions are permeable. Several midrashic sources point to the upper and lower waters as not being as ontologically exclusive as the prayer appears to declare. Employing the verse of the Psalms 42, "The deep calls to the deep," several sources emphasize how the upper and lower waters move toward each other, desire to combine, or do combine in the form of rain falling to earth. Thus, *Midrash Rabbah* Genesis, 13:13, portrays the upper waters as male and the lower waters as female. And other sources speak of rainwater penetrating far under the ground to "the waters of the deep." If so, then the appearance of separation is deceptive and ultimately overcome.

Also, the boundary between day and night is murky, with a zone of time in between that can be either day or night. This time is mixed with light and darkness, a "between" time, in Jewish law. One midrashic source says that in the winter the night borrows from the day, and in the summer the day then borrows from the night (*Midrash Tanhuma*, Mishpatim, 15). Let this cooperative note be applied to the other distinctions.

Indeed the very distinction between the Sabbath and the weekdays becomes blurred in Hasidic circles. Rabbi Yehudah Aryeh Leib Alter (1847–1905) wrote about the concept of "keeping the Sabbath" as referring to holding on to the Sabbath and taking it with you into the days of the week. A Jew is enjoined not to let go of the Sabbath when the Sabbath lets go of him or her.[9] A famous Hasidic tale tells of the brothers, Rabbi Elimelech of Lizhensk (1717–1786) and Rabbi Meshulam Zusha of Anipoli (1718-1800), who feared that their sense of spiritual exhilaration on the Sabbath might be nothing more than their great enjoyment of the special foods and the dressing up with fancy clothes with great pomp. So they celebrated the Sabbath evening feast on that Tuesday evening, with all the beautiful clothing and special dishes, to test whether what they felt on the Sabbath was the enjoyment of those or was a true spiritual soaring. Sadly, their hearts fell when they had the same experience on Tuesday evening that they always had on the Sabbath eve! Their despondency lasted only until their teacher told them that what they had experienced that Tuesday evening was nothing less than the taste of the Sabbath that seeps into the days of the week! Overjoyed, they met the next Friday evening with renewed confidence. There was no chasm of distinction between the Sabbath and the days of the week.

Seen in this way, the *havdalah* prayer receives a different cast. God might have created the Sabbath as ostensibly separate from the weekdays, but we are capable of seeing through that separation to an underlying dynamic that challenges it and succeeds in overcoming it. The Sabbath permeates the six days of the week. The difference between the holy and profane is not one between exclusive contrasts.

---

9   Rabbi Yehudah Aryeh Leib Alter, *Sfat Emet* (Israel: 1971), Volume 2, 68, and *inter alia*.

Just so, the "distinction" between Jews and Gentiles need not be as ontologically severe as the *havdalah* at first sight implies. Here we can use (part of) a commentary by Rabbi Chaim ben Attar (1696-1742) who declares that if the Torah had said that God had separated *the Gentiles from the Jews*, that would have implied an abandoning of the Gentiles into an unbridgeable ontological gap. Instead, the Bible says that God separated *the Jews from the Gentiles*, which, to this Rabbi, has no such implication.[10] To Rabbi Attar, the gap is bridged by the fact that a non-Jew can convert and become a Jew. For me, the non-Jew being able to hear God's call and authentically respond bridges the gap.

My wholesale approach to this and similar prayers is that all references to non-Jews in the prayers be understood as referring to members of pagan cultures of long ago. It was in the time of such cultures that the Jews were "separated" out as God's Chosen People. Hence, all prayers are to refer back to foundational times when Jews were distinguished from the surrounding pagans. In order to raise this interpretation to general consciousness, it will be necessary to take steps to insure that these prayers do not leak out to include reference to contemporary, non-pagan Gentiles. A further move in a wholesale reinterpretation should include taking the pagans of old as being in addition forces within each of us that require deep inner transformation away from personal "paganism" to personal love of God and of other humans. The recognition that in each Jew there lurks an Idol Worshiper who must be radically transformed is redemptive of an attitude that sees evil and alienation from God only outside of us, especially in other nations.

This sampling of some traditional Jewish liturgy points to a direction of reinterpretation consonant with God's love of the Jewish people as a figure of God's love for all. The past is to move into the future.

---

10   Rabbi *Chaim ben Attar, Or Hahayim on Deuteronomy 33:3.*

Conclusion

God chooses the Jews for God to display through them God's love for all of humankind, while inviting the non-Jews to come to God in freedom. The Jews can play a role in the success of God's aim of drawing all of humanity to God. When God shows love to the Jewish people and they reciprocate that love to God, then the Jews display for the world how much they cherish God's love. Thereby, the Jews enhance the power of the image of God's love for the Jews, and by inference, for the world. When the Jews do not reciprocate, they weaken the image of God's love by failing to take it up and celebrating it. They therefore cheapen God's love as a good to yearn for and gain. Here I would employ a rabbinic saying on Isaiah 43:10, "You are my witnesses, says the Lord, and I am God," to drive home my point:

> Rabbi Shimon bar Yochai said: If you are my witnesses, then I am God, but if you are not my witnesses, then, as it were, I am not God. (*Pesikta deRav Kahana*, 12)

When the Jews witness to God they strengthen the impact of the original divine choice of the Jews. When the Jews fail to reciprocate God's love, God is moved to the shadows. Hence, the Jews' demonstration of their love of God becomes a derivative figure of humanity's love of God and of the promise of mutuality of love between God and a person.

The proper response of the Jews to God is to accept God as sovereign in the world, to acknowledge the world's dependence upon God, and respond positively to God's wishes for us. We Jews declare God's sovereignty in the *Shema* declaration: "Listen Israel: The Lord is our God, the Lord is One;" We recognize our dependence upon God in prayer, as for example when we thank God for "our lives which are entrusted into Your hand, for our souls which are placed in your charge, for Your miracles which are with us every day;" and respond positively to God when we keep God's commandments.

If our response to God is to further God's desire that God's love of us be a figure for all of humanity, we do best to act explicitly for God. By acting explicitly for God, we enliven the sense of mutuality between humanity and God for all to see. And if our response to God is to further God's desire that God's love of us be a figure for all of humanity, our primary commitment should be to God as filtered *through* our Judaism. Our primary commitment must not be to Judaism itself, but to God.

R. Mordecai Joseph Leiner of Izbica (1800-1854), in his two volume *Mei HaShiloach*, speaks ubiquitously of transgressing the Law for God's sake. While the idea is quite complex, essentially it boils down to the idea that in a given concrete situation God might want a person to transgress—then and there—God's standing Law. I do not take the "Izbicer" seriously to be advocating pious sinning in reality. R. Mordecai Joseph's endorsement of pious transgression is colored by his repeated cautions for extreme care before deciding to act on what strikes you as God's exceptional will for you now. The Izbicer forcefully demands the need to scrutinize yourself "seven times seventy" times before acting on what you take to be God's will, if it should contradict the laws of the Torah. I suggest that when writing about sinning at God's behest, the Izbicer never envisioned anybody ("God forbid!") actually *engaging* in pious transgression. Rather, what was important to the Izbicer was that a person simply be able to *imagine* herself sinning for God. In R. Mordecai Joseph's mind, the person who cannot ever imagine the sheer *possibility* of God's wanting her to sin against the "system," is found out to hold a primary commitment to the *system*, and not to God. In contrast, one who recognizes the sheer possibility of her sinning at God's directive will always keep in mind that God is the source and the *telos* of the "system." She will thus be nurturing an ultimate relationship to God, and not to the system itself. If I am right, then R. Mordecai Joseph wrote about pious transgression as a device to deepen the classic Hasidic theme of *devekut*, or cleaving, to God. Jewish chosenness requires precisely this commitment to God's own self.[1]

---

1   For an extensive presentation of Rabbi Leiner's thought, see Shaul Magid, *Hasidism on the Margin: Reconciliation, Antinomianism, and Messianism in Izbica/Radzin Hasidism* (Madison: University of Wisconsin Press, 2003). See also Jerome Gellman, *The Fear, the Trembling, and the Fire: Kierkegaard and Hasidic Masters on the Binding of Isaac* (Lanham, MD: University Press of America, 1994), Chapters 2 and 3; and Jerome Gellman, *Abraham! Abraham! Kierkegaard and the Hasidim on the Binding of Isaac* (London: Ashgate Publishers, 2003), Chapters 3-6. See also: Morris M. Feierstein, *All is in the Hands of Heaven: The Teachings of Rabbi Mordecai Joseph Leiner of Izbica*, Revised Edition (Piscataway, NJ: Gorgias Press, 2005).

Devotion to the Torah can become idol worship if not subsumed under a primary relationship to God. This occurs when its forms are frozen into shapes no longer apt for serving God. Such is the motivation of the present work—that to hold on to old concepts of the Jews as the chosen people and not to go forward constitutes a fixation on Torah that does not join together easily with contemporary possibilities of serving God.

The Jews can advance God's purposes in having chosen them by acting in ways *congruent* with God's will, as best we can understand.

In addition, as I have already written, when a Jew loves a non-Jew, when appropriate, as a Jew and in the name of Judaism, the love the Jew grants is God's love breaking into the natural order for the non-Jew. And when the Jew loves in that way, the possibility of the love being received as God's love is made real. Love of the non-Jew by a Jew carries the message of the Jews as the chosen people outward to those to be benefitted by God's enduring love.

The obligations of the Jews to confirm God's purpose in choosing them by their reciprocation of God's love and their love of the Other have become acute with the creation of the country of Israel and with the existence of a collective center of Jewish life for the first time in two millennia. In the scattered existence of exile, Jewish worship of God centered on private and local forms. With the existence of the State of Israel, these forms have been supplemented by a broad field of potential forms of worship of God, those embodied in state and government institutions. Personal and local worship too become impacted and reshaped by the reality of a Jewish society. In addition, concurrent with the existence of a Jewish state come the pressures of modernity and the need for rethinking Jewish religiosity so as to be a proper vehicle in all respects of serving God. In this way, the corporate nation of the Jews once again appears on the world stage to figure as an example of a mutual love between a nation and God.

The State of Israel as well affords a collective, societal opportunity of love for the non-Jew that barely existed for two thousand years. The collective expression of love by the country of Israel surpasses individual acts of love in representing acts done in the name of the Jewish people and their religious heritage. For me, a source of tragic lament is that my country is entangled in a mesh of warfare and enmity that does not free her sufficiently to act out her chosenness.

It is my fervent prayer that as time goes by God will be able to say with more confidence, "You are my witnesses, and I am God." Yet, the chosenness of the Jews does not depend on our reciprocation of God's overwhelming love to us. As a Midrash states: "When God is angry at the Jewish people God is endeared to them. How much more so when God is feeling love for them!" (Bamidbar Rabbah, 2:15). So it is for all humanity.

Bibliography

Alston, William P. "Realism and the Christian Faith," *International Journal for Philosophy of Religion*, 38 (1995): 37-60.

Alter, R. Yehudah Aryeh Leib. *Sfat Emet*. Israel, 1971.

Ashlag, Yehuda. *Matan Torah* (Hebrew). Bnei Brak: Or Baruch Shalom, 2007.

Cassuto, Umberto. *A Commentary on the Book of Exodus*. Jerusalem: Magnes Publishing House, 1967.

Cheng, Hsueh-Li. "Nāgārjuna's Approach to the Problem of the Existence of God," *Religious Studies*, 12 (1976): 207-216.

Chisholm, Roderick M. *The Foundations of Knowing*. Minneapolis: University of Minnesota Press, 1982.

Clifford, William. *Lectures and Essays*, edited by Leslie Stephen and Frederick Pollock. London: Macmillan, 1879.

Dorff, Elliot N. *To Do the Right and the Good: A Jewish Approach to Modern Social Ethics*. Philadelphia: Jewish Publication Society, 2002.

_____. *The Way Into Tikkun Olam: Repairing the World*. Woodstock, VT: Jewish Lights, 2005.

Eldrege, Niles and Stephen Jay Gould. "Punctuated Equilibria: An Alternative to Phyletic Gradualism." In *Models in Paleobiology*, edited by T. J. M. Schopf, 82-115. San Francisco: Freeman, Cooper, and Co., 1972.

Eshleman, Andrew S. "Can an Atheist Believe in God?" *Religious Studies*, 41 (2005): 183–199.

_____. "Religious Fictionalism Defended: Reply to Cordy," *Religious Studies*, 46 (2010): 91-96.

Evans, C. Stephen. *Natural Signs and Knowledge of God, A New Look at Theistic Arguments*. New York: Oxford University Press, 2010.

Feierstein, Morris M. *All Is in the Hands of Heaven, The Teachings of Rabbi Mordecai Joseph Leiner of Izbica* (Revised Edition). Piscataway, NJ: Gorgias Press, 2005.

Fine, Lawrence. "Tikkun: A Lurianic Motif in Contemporary Jewish Thought." In *Ancient Israel to Modern Judaism IV*, edited by Jacob Neusner, Ernest S. Frerichs, and Nahum M. Sarna, 35-53. Atlanta: Scholars Press, 1989.

Finkelstein, Israel. *The Bible Unearthed: Archeology's New Vision of Ancient Israel and the Origin of its Sacred Texts.* New York: Simon and Schuster, 2002.

Firestone, Reuven. *Who are the Real Chosen People: The Meaning of Chosenness in Judaism, Christianity, and Islam.* Woodstock, VT.: Skylight Paths Publishing, 2008.

Freedman, David Noel. *The Nine Commandments.* New York: Doubleday, 2000.

Friedman, Yohanan. *Tolerance and Coercion in Islam, Interfaith Relations in the Muslim Tradition.* Cambridge: Cambridge University, 2003.

Frerichs, Ernest S. and Leonard H. Lesko, editors. *Exodus: The Egyptian Evidence.* Winona Lake, IN: Eisenbrauns, 1997.

Frymer-Kensky, Tikva. "The Strange Case of the Sucted Sotah," *Vetus Testamentum,* 34 (1984): 11-26.

Gellman, Jerome. *Abraham! Abraham! Kierkegaard and the Hasidim on the Binding of Isaac.* London: Ashgate Publishers, 2003.

_____, "Judaism and Buddhism." In *Judaism and World Religions*, edited by Alon Goshen-Gottstein and Eugene Korn. Littman Library: Oxford University Press, 2012.

_____. *The Fear, the Trembling, and the Fire: Kierkegaard and Hasidic Masters on the Binding of Isaac.* Lanham, MD: University Press of America, 1994.

_____. "Jewish Mysticism and Morality: Kabbalah and its Ontological Dualities," *Archiv fur Religiongeschichte,* 9, (2008): 23-36.

Gnuse, Robert Karl. *No Other Gods, Emergent Monotheism in Israel.* Sheffield, England: Sheffield Academic Press, 1997.

Golden, Mark. "Demography and the Exposure of Girls at Athens," *Phoenix,* 35 (1981): 316-331.

Goldman, Alvin. *Knowledge in a Social World.* Oxford: Oxford University, 1999.

The Gospel of Ramakrishna. Translated by Swami Nikhilananda. Mylapore: Sri Ramakrishna Math, 1964.

Greenberg, Irving. "Cloud of Smoke, Pillar of Fire: Judaism, Christianity, and Modernity after the Holocaust." In *Auschwitz: Beginning of a New Era?* edited by E. Fleischner, 1-55. New York: Ktav Publishing House 1977.

Halamish, Moshe. "Some Acts Concerning the Question of the Relationship of the Kabbalists to the Nations of the World." In *Israeli Philosophy* (Hebrew), edited by Asa Kasher and Moshe Halamish, 49-71. Ramat-Aviv: Papyrus Publishing, 1983.

Halbertal, Moshe. "'Ones Possessed of Religion': Religious Tolerance in the Teachings of the Meiri," *The Edah Journal*, 1 (2001).

Halivni, David Weiss. *Breaking the Tablets: Jewish Theology After the Shoah*. Lanham, MD: Rowman and Littlefield Publishers, 2007.

Harkins, Angela Kim. "Biblical and Historical Perspectives on 'the People of God.'" In *Transforming Relations: Essays on Jews and Christians throughout History*, In Honor of Michael E. Signer, edited by Franklin T. Harkins, 319-339. Notre Dame, IN: University of Notre Dame Press, 2010.

Hartshorne, Charles. *Omnipotence and Other Theological Mistakes*. Albany: State University of New York, 1984.

Hayes, Richard P. "Principled Atheism in the Buddhist Scholastic Tradition," *Journal of Indian Philosophy*, 16 (1988): 5-28.

Hepburn, Ronald W. "From World to God," *Mind*, 72 (1963): 40-50.

Hick, John. *An Interpretation of Religion: Human Responses to the Transcendent*. New York: Macmillan, 1989.

Hick, John. *Faith and Knowledge*. Ithaca: Cornell University Press, 1957.

Hirshman, Marc. *Torah for All Persons: A Universal Approach in Tanaitic Literature and Its Relationship to Wisdom of the Nations* (Hebrew). Israel: Israel Ministry of Defense, 1999.

James, William. *The Will to Believe and Other Essays in Popular Philosophy, and Human Immortality*. New York: Dover Publications, 1956.

Jospe, Raphael "Teaching Yehuda Halevi: Defining and Shattering Myths in Jewish Philosophy." In *Paradigms in Jewish Philosophy*, edited by Raphael Jospe, 112-128. Danvers, MA: Associated University Presses, 1997.

Kaminsky, Joel S. *Yet I Loved Jacob: Reclaiming the Biblical Concept of Election*. Nashville: Abingdon Press, 2007.

Katz, Jacob. *Tradition and Crisis: Jewish Society at the End of the Middle Ages*. New York: Schoken Books, 1971.

Katz, Steven T. editor. *The Impact of the Holocaust on Jewish Theology*. New York and London: New York University Press, 2005.

Kaufman, William E. *The Evolving God in Jewish Process Theology*. Lewiston, NY: Edwin Mellen Press, 1997.

Kellner, Menachem. "Chosenness, Not Chauvinism: Maimonides on the Chosen People." In *A People Apart, Chosenness and Ritual in Jewish Philosophical Thought,* edited by Daniel H. Frank. Albany: State University of New York Press, 1995.

_____. *Maimonides on Judaism and the Jewish People*. Albany: State University of New York Press, 1991.

Kierkegaard, Søren. *Fear and Trembling.* Princeton: Princeton University Press, 1970.

_____. *Philosophical Fragments.*

_____. *Works of Love,* Edited and Translated with Introduction by Howard V. Hong and Edna H. Hong. Princeton: Princeton University Press, 1995.

Kogan, Michael S. *Opening the Covenant: A Jewish Theology of Christianity.* New York: Oxford University Press, 2008.

Kook, Abraham Isaac. *Orot Haemunah.* Jerusalem: Mosad Harav Kook, 1995.

Kreisel, Howard. *Prophecy: The History of an Idea in Medieval Jewish Philosophy.* Dordrecht, The Netherlands: Kluwer Academic Publishers, 2001.

Kugel, James L. *How to Read the Bible: A Guide to Scripture, Then and Now.* New York: Free Press, 2007.

Kung, Hans. *The Church.* Garden City: Image Books, 1976.

Kvanvig, Jonathan L. "Religious Pluralism and the Buridan's Ass Paradox," *European Journal for Philosophy of Religion,* 1 (2009): 1-26.

Langer, Ruth. *Cursing the Christians? A History of the Birkat HaMinim.* New York: Oxford University Press, 2011.

Lasker, Daniel, "Tradition and Innovation in Maimonides' Attitude toward Other Religions." In *Maimonides after 800 Years: Essays on*

Maimonides and His Influence, edited by Jay M. Harris, 167-182. Cambridge, MA and London: Harvard University Press, 2007.

Magid, Shaul. *Hasidism on the Margin, Reconciliation, Antinomianism, and Messianism in Izbica/Radzin Hasidism.* Madison: University of Wisconsin Press, 2003.

McKim, Robert. *On Religious Diversity.* Oxford: Oxford University Press, 2012.

Moser, Paul K. *The Elusive God: Reorienting Religious Epistemology.* Cambridge: Cambridge University Press, 2008.

Murray, Michael. "Coercion and the Hiddenness of God," *American Philosophical Quarterly,* 30 (1993): 27-38.

Novak, David. *The Election of Israel: The Idea of the Chosen People.* Cambridge: Cambridge University Press, 1995.

_____. *The Image of the Non-Jew in Judaism: An Historical and Constructive Study of the Noahide Laws.* Lewiston, NY: Edwin Mellen Press, 1983.

Plaskow, Judith. *Standing Again at Sinai: Judaism from a Feminist Perspective.* San Francisco: Harper Collins, 1991.

Plantinga, Alvin. *Warranted Christian Belief.* Oxford: Oxford University Press, 2000.

Rosenzeweig, Franz. *Star of Redemption.* Translated by Barbara E. Galli. Madison: University of Wisconsin Press, 2005.

Ross, Tamar. *Expanding the Palace of Torah: Orthodoxy and Feminism.* Waltham, MA: Brandeis University Press, 2004.

Sacks, Jonathan. *The Dignity of Difference: How to Avoid the Clash of Civilizations.* London: Continuum Books, 2002.

Shapiro, Marc. "Of Books and Bans," *The Edah Journal,* 3 (1992/93): 1-16.

Shatz, David, Chaim I. Waxman and Nathan J. Diament, editors. *Tikkun Olam: Social Responsibility in Jewish Thought and Law.* Northvale, NJ and London: Jason Aronson, 1997.

Schuon, Frithjof. *The Transcendent Unity of Religions.* Wheaten, IL: Theosophical Publishing House, 1984.

Schimmel, Annemarie. *Mystical Dimensions of Islam.* Chapel Hill: University of North Carolina, 1975.

Schwartz, Dov. *Challenge and Crisis in Rabbi Kook's Circle* (Hebrew). Tel-Aviv: Am Oved, 2001.

Smith, Mark S. *The Memoirs of God: History, Memory, and the Experience of God in Ancient Israel.* Minneapolis: Fortress Press, 2004.

Smith, William Robertson. *Lectures on the Religion of the Semites: The Fundamental Institutions*, Third Edition. New York: Ktav Publishing House, 1969.

Sperber, Daniel. *On Changes in Jewish Liturgy: Options and Limitations.* Jerusalem and New York: Urim Publications, 2010.

Spinoza, Baruch. *Tractatus Theologico-Politicus.* Leiden and New York: E. J. Brill, 1989.

Tishby, Isaiah. *The Theory of Evil in Lurianic Kabbalah* (Hebrew). Jerusalem: Magnes Press, 1993/4.

Wijnhoven, Jochanan H. A. "The *Zohar* and the Proselyte," in *Texts and Responses: Studies Presented to Nahum N. Glatzer on the Occasion of his Seventieth Birthday*, edited by Michael A. Fishbane and Paul R. Flohr, 120-140. Leidin: E. J. Brill, 1975.

Wyschogrod, Michael. *The Body of Faith, Judaism as Corporeal Election.* Minneapolis: Seabury Press, 1983.

Yerushalmi, Yosef Hayim. *Zakhor: Jewish History and Jewish Memory.* Seattle and London: University of Washington Press, 1982.

Index

CPSIA information can be obtained at www.ICGtesting.com
Printed in the USA
LVOW03*1738040915

452615LV00006B/23/P